MznLnx

Missing Links Exam Preps

Exam Prep for

Leadership: Enhancing the Lessons of Experience

Hughes, Ginnett, & Curphy, 6th Edition

The MznLnx Exam Prep is your link from the texbook and lecture to your exams.
The MznLnx Exam Preps are unauthorized and comprehensive reviews of your textbooks.

All material provided by MznLnx and Rico Publications (c) 2010
Textbook publishers and textbook authors do not particpate in or contribute to these reviews.

MznLnx

Rico
Publications

Exam Prep for Leadership: Enhancing the Lessons of Experience
6th Edition
Hughes, Ginnett, & Curphy

Publisher: Raymond Houge
Assistant Editor: Michael Rouger
Text and Cover Designer: Lisa Buckner
Marketing Manager: Sara Swagger
Project Manager, Editorial Production: Jerry Emerson
Art Director: Vernon Lowerui

Product Manager: Dave Mason
Editorial Assitant: Rachel Guzmanji
Pedagogy: Debra Long
Cover Image: Jim Reed/Getty Images
Text and Cover Printer: City Printing, Inc.
Compositor: Media Mix, Inc.

(c) 2010 Rico Publications
ALL RIGHTS RESERVED. No part of this work covered by the copyright may be reproduced or used in any form or by an means--graphic, electronic, or mechanical, including photocopying, recording, taping, Web distribution, information storage, and retrieval systems, or in any other manner--without the written permission of the publisher.

Printed in the United States
ISBN:

For more information about our products, contact us at:
Dave.Mason@RicoPublications.com

For permission to use material from this text or product, submit a request online to:
Dave.Mason@RicoPublications.com

Contents

CHAPTER 1
Leadership Is Everyone's Business — 1

CHAPTER 2
Leadership Involves an Interaction — 2

CHAPTER 3
Leadership Is Developed through Education and Experience — 8

CHAPTER 4
Assessing Leadership and Measuring Its Effects — 15

CHAPTER 5
Power and Influence — 24

CHAPTER 6
Leadership and Values — 30

CHAPTER 7
Leadership Traits — 37

CHAPTER 8
Leadership Behavior — 44

CHAPTER 9
Motivation, Satisfaction, and Performance — 57

CHAPTER 10
Groups, Teams and Their Leadership — 70

CHAPTER 11
Characteristics of the Situation — 86

CHAPTER 12
Contingency Theories of Leadership — 96

CHAPTER 13
Leadership and Change — 100

ANSWER KEY — 111

TO THE STUDENT

COMPREHENSIVE

The *MznLnx* Exam Prep series is designed to help you pass your exams. Editors at MznLnx review your textbooks and then prepare these practice exams to help you master the textbook material. Unlike study guides, workbooks, and practice tests provided by the texbook publisher and textbook authors, *MznLnx* gives you **all** of the material in each chapter in exam form, not just samples, so you can be sure to nail your exam.

MECHANICAL

The MznLnx Exam Prep series creates exams that will help you learn the subject matter as well as test you on your understanding. Each question is designed to help you master the concept. Just working through the exams, you gain an understanding of the subject--its a simple mechanical process that produces success.

INTEGRATED STUDY GUIDE AND REVIEW

MznLnx is not just a set of exams designed to test you, its also a comprehensive review of the subject content. Each exam question is also a review of the concept, making sure that you will get the answer correct without having to go to other sources of material. You learn as you go! Its the easiest way to pass an exam.

HUMOR

Studying can be tedious and dry. MznLnx's instructional design includes moderate humor within the exam questions on occassion, to break the tedium and revitalize the brain

Chapter 1. Leadership Is Everyone's Business

1. The sociologist Max Weber defined _____ as 'resting on devotion to the exceptional sanctity, heroism or exemplary character of an individual person, and of the normative patterns or order revealed or ordained by him.' _____ is one of three forms of authority laid out in Weber's tripartite classification of authority, the other two being traditional authority and rational-legal authority. The concept has acquired wide usage among sociologists.

   In his writings about _____, Weber applies the term charisma to 'a certain quality of an individual personality, by virtue of which he is set apart from ordinary men and treated as endowed with supernatural, superhuman, or at least specifically exceptional powers or qualities.

   a. 33 Strategies of War
   b. 28-hour day
   c. 1990 Clean Air Act
   d. Charismatic authority

2. _____ is a term used to classify a group leadership theories that inquire the interactions between leaders and followers. A transactional leader focuses more on a series of 'transactions'. This person is interested in looking out for oneself, having exchange benefits with their subordinates and clarify a sense of duty with rewards and punishments to reach goals.
   a. Transactional leadership
   b. Reflective listening
   c. Care perspective
   d. Negative affectivity

3. _____ is a leadership style that defines as leadership that creates voluble and positive change in the followers. A transformational leader focuses on 'transforming' others to help each other, to look out for each other, be encouraging, harmonious, and look out for the organization as a whole. In this leadership, the leader enhances the motivation, moral and performance of his follower group.
   a. Milgram experiment
   b. Transformational leadership
   c. Need for affiliation
   d. Subpersonality

4. _____ is acquiring new knowledge, behaviors, skills, values, preferences or understanding, and may involve synthesizing different types of information. The ability to learn is possessed by humans, animals and some machines. Progress over time tends to follow _____ curves.
   a. Learning cycle
   b. Learning curve
   c. Meta learning
   d. Learning

Chapter 2. Leadership Involves an Interaction

1. _____ is the state achieved by coming together, the state of agreement. The Latin congruere means to come together, agree. As an abstract term, _____ means similarity between objects.
   a. The Goodyear Tire ' Rubber Company
   b. Turnover
   c. HMIS
   d. Congruence

2. _____ is the set of reasons that determines one to engage in a particular behavior. The term is generally used for human _____ but, theoretically, it can be used to describe the causes for animal behavior as well
   a. Work behavior
   b. Losada Zone
   c. Motivation
   d. Losada line

3. In sociology, an _____ is a social group towards which an individual feels contempt, opposition, or a desire to compete. Members of _____s may be subject to _____ homogeneity biases, and generally people tend to privilege ingroup members over _____ members in many situations. The term originates from social identity theory.
   a. Androgen receptor
   b. Aneuploidy
   c. Orthologs
   d. Outgroup

4. Social _____ is a social psychological and sociological perspective that explains social change and stability as a process of negotiated exchanges between parties. Social _____ posits that all human relationships are formed by the use of a subjective cost-benefit analysis and the comparison of alternatives. For example, when a person perceives the costs of a relationship as outweighing the perceived benefits, then the theory predicts that the person will choose to leave the relationship.
   a. A Stake in the Outcome
   b. AAAI
   c. A4e
   d. Exchange theory

5. Leadership is one of the primary areas of study, research, and practice in organizational behavior. Leaders often develop relationships with each member of the group that they lead, and _____ explains how those relationships with various members can develop in unique ways.

The _____ of leadership focuses on the two-way relationship between supervisors and subordinates.

a. Light curtains
b. Groups decision making
c. Leader-Member Exchange theory
d. Human Centered Systems

6. _____ is purposeful and reflective judgment about what to believe or what to do in response to observations, experience, verbal or written expressions, or arguments. _____ might involve determining the meaning and significance of what is observed or expressed, or, concerning a given inference or argument, determining whether there is adequate justification to accept the conclusion as true. Hence, Fisher ' Scriven define _____ as 'Skilled, active, interpretation and evaluation of observations, communications, information, and argumentation.' Parker ' Moore define it more narrowly as the careful, deliberate determination of whether one should accept, reject, or suspend judgment about a claim and the degree of confidence with which one accepts or rejects it.
   a. Critical thinking
   b. Succession planning
   c. 1990 Clean Air Act
   d. Virtual team

7. The _____ was created at a 1996 summit meeting of 11 of the world's then-current and former presidents and prime ministers. The first convening of the Council took place in 1997 at Harvard University's Kennedy School of Government. The _____ presently has 37 members - nearly all of the current and former female heads of state and heads of government.
   a. 33 Strategies of War
   b. Council of Women World Leaders
   c. 1990 Clean Air Act
   d. 28-hour day

8. A _____ is a distinction of biological and/or physiological characteristics typically associated with either males or females of a species in general. In the study of humans, socio-political issues arise in classifying whether a sex difference results from the biology of gender
   a. Living wage
   b. Mediation
   c. McJob
   d. Gender difference

9. In economics, the term _____ refers to situations where the advancement of a qualified person within the hierarchy of an organization is stopped at a lower level because of some form of discrimination, most commonly sexism or racism, but since the term was coined, '_____' has also come to describe the limited advancement of the deaf, blind, disabled, aged and sexual minorities. It is an unofficial, invisible barrier that prevents women and minorities from advancing in businesses.

This situation is referred to as a 'ceiling' as there is a limitation blocking upward advancement, and 'glass' (transparent) because the limitation is not immediately apparent and is normally an unwritten and unofficial policy. This invisible barrier continues to exist, even though there are no explicit obstacles keeping minorities from acquiring advanced job positions - there are no advertisements that specifically say 'no minorities hired at this establishment', nor are there any formal orders that say 'minorities are not qualified' - but they do lie beneath the surface.

   a. 28-hour day
   b. 33 Strategies of War
   c. 1990 Clean Air Act
   d. Glass Ceiling

10. _____ is the name applied to two competing management theories. One was developed by Abraham H. Maslow in his book Maslow on Management and the other is Dr. William Ouchi's so-called 'Japanese Management' style popularized during the Asian economic boom of the 1980s. In contrast Theory X, which stated that workers inherently dislike and avoid work and must be driven to it, and Theory Y, which stated that work is natural and can be a source of satisfaction when aimed at higher order human psychological needs, _____ focused on increasing employee loyalty to the company by providing a job for life with a strong focus on the well-being of the employee, both on and off the job.
   a. 28-hour day
   b. 1990 Clean Air Act
   c. 33 Strategies of War
   d. Theory Z

11. The _____ is a self-report inventory created by Harrison Gough and currently published by Consulting Psychologists Press. It was created in a similar manner to the Minnesota Multiphasic Personality Inventory (MMPI), but unlike the MMPI, it is not concerned with maladjustment or clinical diagnosis, but concerned itself with more 'normal' aspects of personality.

The _____ is made up of 434 true-false questions, half of which were taken from the original version of the MMPI.

a. Bogardus Social Distance Scale
b. Robin Hood Morality Test
c. California Psychological Inventory
d. Personality Assessment Inventory

12. _____ is the imitation of some real thing, state of affairs, or process. The act of simulating something generally entails representing certain key characteristics or behaviours of a selected physical or abstract system.

_____ is used in many contexts, including the modeling of natural systems or human systems in order to gain insight into their functioning.

a. 33 Strategies of War
b. Simulation
c. 1990 Clean Air Act
d. 28-hour day

13. In the fields of information science, communication, and industrial design, there is debate over the meaning of Interactivity. In the 'contingency view' of interactivity, there are three levels: Noninteractive, when a message is not related to previous messages; Reactive, when a message is related only to one immediately previous message; and _____, when a message is related to a number of previous messages and to the relationship between them.

Interactivity is similar to the degree of responsiveness, and is examined as a communication process in which each message is related to the previous messages exchanged, and to the relation of those messages to the messages preceding them.

a. Interactive
b. AAAI
c. A Stake in the Outcome
d. A4e

14. A _____ or chief executive is one of the highest-ranking corporate officer (executive) or administrator in charge of total management. An individual selected as President and _____ of a corporation, company, organization, or agency, reports to the board of directors. In internal communication and press releases, many companies capitalize the term and those of other high positions, even when they are not proper nouns.

a. Learning
b. Chief executive officer
c. Questionnaire
d. Bandwagon effect

Chapter 2. Leadership Involves an Interaction

15. _____ is a kind of action that occurs as two or more objects have an effect upon one another. The idea of a two-way effect is essential in the concept of _____, as opposed to a one-way causal effect. A closely related term is interconnectivity, which deals with the _____s of _____s within systems: combinations of many simple _____s can lead to surprising emergent phenomena.

   a. Organizational dissent
   b. Organizational communication
   c. Interpersonal communication
   d. Interaction

16. _____ forms part of thinking. Considered the most complex of all intellectual functions, _____ has been defined as higher-order cognitive process that requires the modulation and control of more routine or fundamental skills. It occurs if an organism or an artificial intelligence system does not know how to proceed from a given state to a desired goal state.

   a. Functional fixedness
   b. Thinking outside the box
   c. 1990 Clean Air Act
   d. Problem solving

17. The sociologist Max Weber defined _____ as 'resting on devotion to the exceptional sanctity, heroism or exemplary character of an individual person, and of the normative patterns or order revealed or ordained by him.' _____ is one of three forms of authority laid out in Weber's tripartite classification of authority, the other two being traditional authority and rational-legal authority. The concept has acquired wide usage among sociologists.

   In his writings about _____, Weber applies the term charisma to 'a certain quality of an individual personality, by virtue of which he is set apart from ordinary men and treated as endowed with supernatural, superhuman, or at least specifically exceptional powers or qualities.

   a. 33 Strategies of War
   b. 28-hour day
   c. 1990 Clean Air Act
   d. Charismatic authority

18. _____ is a term used to classify a group leadership theories that inquire the interactions between leaders and followers. A transactional leader focuses more on a series of 'transactions'. This person is interested in looking out for oneself, having exchange benefits with their subordinates and clarify a sense of duty with rewards and punishments to reach goals.

a. Care perspective
b. Reflective listening
c. Negative affectivity
d. Transactional leadership

19. _____ is a leadership style that defines as leadership that creates voluble and positive change in the followers. A transformational leader focuses on 'transforming' others to help each other, to look out for each other, be encouraging, harmonious, and look out for the organization as a whole. In this leadership, the leader enhances the motivation, moral and performance of his follower group.
   a. Subpersonality
   b. Need for affiliation
   c. Transformational leadership
   d. Milgram experiment

Chapter 3. Leadership Is Developed through Education and Experience

1. More recently organizations have come to understand that leadership can also be developed by strengthening the connection between and alignment of the efforts of individual leaders and the systems through which they influence organizational operations. This has led to a differentiation between leader development and _____. Leader development focuses on the development of the leader, such as the personal attributes desired in a leader, desired ways of behaving, ways of thinking or feeling.
   a. Leadership development
   b. Group process consultation
   c. Pseudoconsensus
   d. Path-goal theory

2. _____ asserts that there is a technique, method, process, activity, incentive or reward that is more effective at delivering a particular outcome than any other technique, method, process, etc. The idea is that with proper processes, checks, and testing, a desired outcome can be delivered with fewer problems and unforeseen complications. _____s can also be defined as the most efficient (least amount of effort) and effective (best results) way of accomplishing a task, based on repeatable procedures that have proven themselves over time for large numbers of people.
   a. Span of control
   b. Contingency Theory
   c. Management by exception
   d. Best practice

3. A _____ is the learned capacity to carry out pre-determined results often with the minimum outlay of time, energy, or both. _____s can often be divided into domain-general and domain-specific _____s. For example, in the domain of work, some general _____s would include time management, teamwork and leadership, self motivation and others, whereas domain-specific _____s would be useful only for a certain job.
   a. 1990 Clean Air Act
   b. Skill
   c. 33 Strategies of War
   d. 28-hour day

4. In the arts and antiques, _____ is the judgment by experts as to the authorship, date, or other aspect of the origin of a work of art or cultural artifact. Works 'attributed' to an artist are more firmly believed to be theirs than those 'ascribed'.

Chapter 3. Leadership Is Developed through Education and Experience

_____ can also mean:

- _____, a concept in copyright law requiring an author to be credited
- Journalism sourcing (or _____), a journalistic practice of attributing information to its source
- _____ (psychology), a concept in psychology whereby people attribute traits and causes to things they observe
- Performance _____, a technique in quantitative finance for explaining the active performance of a portfolio

a. A Stake in the Outcome
b. Attribution
c. Ambition
d. A4e

5. In attribution theory, the _____ is a theory describing cognitive tendency to predominantly over-value dispositional explanations for the observed behaviors of others, thus under-valuing or acknowledging the potentiality of situational attributions or situational explanations for the behavioral motives of others. In other words, people predominantly presume that the actions of others are indicative of the 'kind' of person they are, rather than the kind of situations that compels their behavior. However, the over attribution effect generally does not account for our own ability to self-justify our behaviors; we tend to prefer interpreting our own actions in terms of the situational variables accessible to our awareness.

a. Pygmalion effect
b. Fundamental attribution error
c. Sunk costs
d. Confirmation bias

6. A _____ occurs when people attribute their successes to internal or personal factors but attribute their failures to situational factors beyond their control. The _____ can be seen in the common human tendency to take credit for success but to deny responsibility for failure (Miller ' Ross, 1975.) It may also manifest itself as a tendency for people to evaluate ambiguous information in a way that is beneficial to their interests.

a. Pygmalion effect
b. Self-serving bias
c. Group-serving bias
d. Halo effect

7. _____ is a term used to described a tendency or preference towards a particular perspective, ideology or result, especially when the tendency interferes with the ability to be impartial, unprejudiced, or objective. The term _____ed is used to describe an action, judgment, or other outcome influenced by a prejudged perspective. It is also used to refer to a person or body of people whose actions or judgments exhibit _____.

a. 33 Strategies of War
b. 1990 Clean Air Act
c. Bias
d. 28-hour day

8. A _____ is a prediction that directly or indirectly causes itself to become true, by the very terms of the prophecy itself, due to positive feedback between belief and behavior. Although examples of such prophecies can be found in literature as far back as ancient Greece and ancient India, it is 20th-century sociologist Robert K. Merton who is credited with coining the expression '_____' and formalizing its structure and consequences. In his book Social Theory and Social Structure, Merton gives as a feature of the _____:

In other words, a prophecy declared as truth when it is actually false may sufficiently influence people, either through fear or logical confusion, so that their reactions ultimately fulfill the once-false prophecy.

a. 33 Strategies of War
b. Self-fulfilling prophecy
c. 1990 Clean Air Act
d. 28-hour day

9. _____ is a kind of action that occurs as two or more objects have an effect upon one another. The idea of a two-way effect is essential in the concept of _____, as opposed to a one-way causal effect. A closely related term is interconnectivity, which deals with the _____s of _____s within systems: combinations of many simple _____s can lead to surprising emergent phenomena.
a. Organizational dissent
b. Interpersonal communication
c. Organizational communication
d. Interaction

10. _____ is acquiring new knowledge, behaviors, skills, values, preferences or understanding, and may involve synthesizing different types of information. The ability to learn is possessed by humans, animals and some machines. Progress over time tends to follow _____ curves.
a. Meta learning
b. Learning curve
c. Learning
d. Learning cycle

11. _____ is the imitation of some real thing, state of affairs, or process. The act of simulating something generally entails representing certain key characteristics or behaviours of a selected physical or abstract system.

Chapter 3. Leadership Is Developed through Education and Experience 11

_____ is used in many contexts, including the modeling of natural systems or human systems in order to gain insight into their functioning.

a. Simulation
b. 1990 Clean Air Act
c. 28-hour day
d. 33 Strategies of War

12. There are two types of _____ relationships: formal and informal. Informal relationships develop on their own between partners. Formal _____, on the other hand, refers to assigned relationships, often associated with organizational _____ programs designed to promote employee development or to assist at-risk children and youth.
   a. Management by exception
   b. Mentoring
   c. Force field analysis
   d. Management by objectives

13. _____ is a method of directing, instructing and training a person or group of people, with the aim to achieve some goal or develop specific skills. There are many ways to coach, types of _____ and methods to _____. Direction may include motivational speaking.
   a. Coaching
   b. Co-coaching
   c. 28-hour day
   d. 1990 Clean Air Act

14. In psychology, _____ is a major approach to the study of human personality. Trait theorists are primarily interested in the measurement of traits, which can be defined as habitual patterns of behavior, thought, and emotion. According to this perspective, traits are relatively stable over time, differ among individuals (e.g. some people are outgoing whereas others are shy), and influence behavior.
   a. Trait theory
   b. Groupthink
   c. Positive psychology
   d. Beck Depression Inventory

15. A _____ is a distinction of biological and/or physiological characteristics typically associated with either males or females of a species in general. In the study of humans, socio-political issues arise in classifying whether a sex difference results from the biology of gender

Chapter 3. Leadership Is Developed through Education and Experience

  a. McJob
  b. Living wage
  c. Mediation
  d. Gender difference

16. The sociologist Max Weber defined _____ as 'resting on devotion to the exceptional sanctity, heroism or exemplary character of an individual person, and of the normative patterns or order revealed or ordained by him.' _____ is one of three forms of authority laid out in Weber's tripartite classification of authority, the other two being traditional authority and rational-legal authority. The concept has acquired wide usage among sociologists.

In his writings about _____, Weber applies the term charisma to 'a certain quality of an individual personality, by virtue of which he is set apart from ordinary men and treated as endowed with supernatural, superhuman, or at least specifically exceptional powers or qualities.

  a. Charismatic authority
  b. 28-hour day
  c. 33 Strategies of War
  d. 1990 Clean Air Act

17. _____ is a term used to classify a group leadership theories that inquire the interactions between leaders and followers. A transactional leader focuses more on a series of 'transactions'. This person is interested in looking out for oneself, having exchange benefits with their subordinates and clarify a sense of duty with rewards and punishments to reach goals.
  a. Negative affectivity
  b. Transactional leadership
  c. Care perspective
  d. Reflective listening

18. _____ is a leadership style that defines as leadership that creates voluble and positive change in the followers. A transformational leader focuses on 'transforming' others to help each other, to look out for each other, be encouraging, harmonious, and look out for the organization as a whole. In this leadership, the leader enhances the motivation, moral and performance of his follower group.
  a. Need for affiliation
  b. Subpersonality
  c. Transformational leadership
  d. Milgram experiment

Chapter 3. Leadership Is Developed through Education and Experience 13

19. _____ is the state achieved by coming together, the state of agreement. The Latin congruere means to come together, agree. As an abstract term, _____ means similarity between objects.
   a. The Goodyear Tire ' Rubber Company
   b. HMIS
   c. Congruence
   d. Turnover

20. _____ describes the situation when output from (or information about the result of) an event or phenomenon in the past will influence the same event/phenomenon in the present or future. When an event is part of a chain of cause-and-effect that forms a circuit or loop, then the event is said to 'feed back' into itself.

   _____ is also a synonym for:

   - _____ Signal; the information about the initial event that is the basis for subsequent modification of the event.
   - _____ Loop; the causal path that leads from the initial generation of the _____ signal to the subsequent modification of the event.

   _____ is a mechanism, process or signal that is looped back to control a system within itself. Such a loop is called a _____ loop.

   a. Feedback
   b. Positive feedback
   c. 28-hour day
   d. 1990 Clean Air Act

21. A _____ or chief executive is one of the highest-ranking corporate officer (executive) or administrator in charge of total management. An individual selected as President and _____ of a corporation, company, organization, or agency, reports to the board of directors. In internal communication and press releases, many companies capitalize the term and those of other high positions, even when they are not proper nouns.
   a. Bandwagon effect
   b. Chief executive officer
   c. Questionnaire
   d. Learning

Chapter 3. Leadership Is Developed through Education and Experience

22. A person's _____ is the mental picture, generally of a kind that is quite resistant to change, that depicts not only details that are potentially available to objective investigation by others (height, weight, hair color, sex, I.Q. score, etc.), but also items that have been learned by that person about himself or herself, either from personal experiences or by internalizing the judgments of others. A simple definition of a person's _____ is their answer to this question - 'What do you believe people think about you?' A more technical term for _____ that is commonly used by social and cognitive psychologists is self-schema. Like any schema, self-schemas store information and influence the way we think and remember.
   a. 1990 Clean Air Act
   b. 28-hour day
   c. 33 Strategies of War
   d. Self image

Chapter 4. Assessing Leadership and Measuring Its Effects

1. _____ is a leadership style that defines as leadership that creates voluble and positive change in the followers. A transformational leader focuses on 'transforming' others to help each other, to look out for each other, be encouraging, harmonious, and look out for the organization as a whole. In this leadership, the leader enhances the motivation, moral and performance of his follower group.

    a. Milgram experiment
    b. Transformational leadership
    c. Need for affiliation
    d. Subpersonality

2. In probability and statistics, _____ generally refers to the (base) class probabilities unconditioned on featural evidence, frequently also known as prior probabilities. For example, if it were the case that 1% of the public are 'medical professionals' and 99% of the public are not 'medical professionals,' then the _____s in this case are 1% and 99%, respectively.

    Naturally, in assessing the probability that a given individual is a member of a particular class, we must account for other information besides the _____.

    a. 28-hour day
    b. 33 Strategies of War
    c. 1990 Clean Air Act
    d. Base rate

3. _____ is the discipline of dealing with and avoiding risks. It is a discipline that involves preparing for disaster before it occurs, disaster response (e.g. emergency evacuation, quarantine, mass decontamination, etc.), as well as supporting, and rebuilding society after natural or human-made disasters have occurred. In general, any _____ is the continuous process by which all individuals, groups, and communities manage hazards in an effort to avoid or ameliorate the impact of disasters resulting from the hazards.

    a. Emergency Management
    b. International Maritime Dangerous Goods Code
    c. A4e
    d. A Stake in the Outcome

4. The phrase _____ refers to the aspect of corporate strategy, corporate finance and management dealing with the buying, selling and combining of different companies that can aid, finance, or help a growing company in a given industry grow rapidly without having to create another business entity.

    An acquisition, also known as a takeover or a buyout, is the buying of one company (the 'target') by another. An acquisition may be friendly or hostile.

a. Political economy
b. 1990 Clean Air Act
c. Mergers and Acquisitions
d. 28-hour day

5. The phrase _____ and acquisitions refers to the aspect of corporate strategy, corporate finance and management dealing with the buying, selling and combining of different companies that can aid, finance, or help a growing company in a given industry grow rapidly without having to create another business entity.

An acquisition, also known as a takeover or a buyout, is the buying of one company (the 'target') by another. An acquisition may be friendly or hostile.

a. 28-hour day
b. Political economy
c. Mergers
d. 1990 Clean Air Act

6. A _____ or chief executive is one of the highest-ranking corporate officer (executive) or administrator in charge of total management. An individual selected as President and _____ of a corporation, company, organization, or agency, reports to the board of directors. In internal communication and press releases, many companies capitalize the term and those of other high positions, even when they are not proper nouns.
a. Questionnaire
b. Bandwagon effect
c. Learning
d. Chief executive officer

7. _____ is a term which portrays a generation born during the middle part of the 20th Century. The birth years of the _____ are the subject of controversy. Historically, everyone born during the post-World War II demographic boom in births was called part of the _____.
a. Baby Boom Generation
b. Wal-Mart
c. Adam Smith
d. Abraham Harold Maslow

8. A _____ is the learned capacity to carry out pre-determined results often with the minimum outlay of time, energy, or both. _____s can often be divided into domain-general and domain-specific _____s. For example, in the domain of work, some general _____s would include time management, teamwork and leadership, self motivation and others, whereas domain-specific _____s would be useful only for a certain job.

Chapter 4. Assessing Leadership and Measuring Its Effects

a. 1990 Clean Air Act
b. 33 Strategies of War
c. 28-hour day
d. Skill

9. The _____ is a term coined by Steven Hankin of McKinsey ' Company in 1997, and a book by Ed Michaels, Helen Handfield-Jones, and Beth Axelrod, Harvard Business Press, 2001 ISBN 1578514592, ISBN 9781578514595. The _____ refers to an increasingly competitive landscape for recruiting and retaining talented employees. In the book, Michaels, et al, describe not a set of superior Human Resources processes, but a mindset that emphasizes the importance of talent to the success of organizations.

a. Personality-Job Fit Theory
b. War for Talent
c. Talent Management Systems
d. Bradford Factor

10. _____ refers to the process of developing and integrating new workers, developing and retaining current workers, and attracting highly skilled workers to work for your company. _____ in this context does not refer to the management of entertainers

a. Human resource consulting
b. Separation of duties
c. Personnel management
d. Talent management

11. The _____, or 'Strategic Human Capital Management Applications', are the next-generation extensions of traditional Human Resource Management Systems (HRMS.)

Whereas traditional HRMS and ERP systems focus primarily on transaction processing and the administration of basic human resources processes such as personnel administration, payroll, time management, etc., _____ focus on providing strategic assistance to organizations in the accomplishment of long-term enterprise goals with respect to talent, or human capital. _____ may also be referred to as/or paired with an Applicant Tracking System (ATS) in either standalone application or as a suite of products.

a. War for talent
b. Contextual performance
c. Talent management systems
d. Job knowledge

Chapter 4. Assessing Leadership and Measuring Its Effects

12. _____ Stores, Inc. is an American public corporation that runs a chain of large, discount department stores. It is the world's largest public corporation by revenue, according to the 2008 Fortune Global 500.
    a. Abraham Harold Maslow
    b. William Edwards Deming
    c. Adam Smith
    d. Wal-Mart

13. _____ involves having senior executives periodically review their top executives and those in the next lower level to determine several backups for each senior position. This is important because it often takes years of grooming to develop effective senior managers. There is a critical shortage in companies of middle and top leaders for the next five years.
    a. 1990 Clean Air Act
    b. Succession planning
    c. Risk management
    d. Virtual team

14. _____ asserts that there is a technique, method, process, activity, incentive or reward that is more effective at delivering a particular outcome than any other technique, method, process, etc. The idea is that with proper processes, checks, and testing, a desired outcome can be delivered with fewer problems and unforeseen complications. _____s can also be defined as the most efficient (least amount of effort) and effective (best results) way of accomplishing a task, based on repeatable procedures that have proven themselves over time for large numbers of people.
    a. Contingency Theory
    b. Management by exception
    c. Best practice
    d. Span of control

15. _____ is a term used to collectively describe topics relating to the operations of firms with interests in multiple countries. Such firms are sometimes called multinational corporations . Well known MNCs include fast food companies McDonald's and Yum Brands, vehicle manufacturers such as General Motors and Toyota, consumer electronics companies like Samsung, LG and Sony, and energy companies such as ExxonMobil and BP.
    a. AAAI
    b. A4e
    c. A Stake in the Outcome
    d. International business

Chapter 4. Assessing Leadership and Measuring Its Effects

16. In economics, the term _____ refers to situations where the advancement of a qualified person within the hierarchy of an organization is stopped at a lower level because of some form of discrimination, most commonly sexism or racism, but since the term was coined, '_____' has also come to describe the limited advancement of the deaf, blind, disabled, aged and sexual minorities.It is an unofficial, invisible barrier that prevents women and minorities from advancing in businesses.

This situation is referred to as a 'ceiling' as there is a limitation blocking upward advancement, and 'glass' (transparent) because the limitation is not immediately apparent and is normally an unwritten and unofficial policy. This invisible barrier continues to exist, even though there are no explicit obstacles keeping minorities from acquiring advanced job positions - there are no advertisements that specifically say 'no minorities hired at this establishment', nor are there any formal orders that say 'minorities are not qualified' - but they do lie beneath the surface.

a. 1990 Clean Air Act
b. Glass ceiling
c. 33 Strategies of War
d. 28-hour day

17. A _____ is a quantitative research method commonly employed in survey research. The aim of this approach is to ensure that each interviewee is presented with exactly the same questions in the same order. This ensures that answers can be reliably aggregated and that comparisons can be made with confidence between sample subgroups or between different survey periods.

a. 28-hour day
b. Structured interview
c. 1990 Clean Air Act
d. Questionnaire

18. _____ are a method of interviews where questions can be changed or adapted to meet the respondent's intelligence, understanding or belief. Unlike a structured interview they do not offer a limited, pre-set range of answers for a respondent to choose, but instead advocate listening to how each individual person responds to the question.

The method to gather information using this technique is fairly limited, for example most surveys that are carried out via telephone or even in person tend to follow a structured method.

a. A4e
b. A Stake in the Outcome
c. AAAI
d. Unstructured interviews

Chapter 4. Assessing Leadership and Measuring Its Effects

19. Social _____ is a social psychological and sociological perspective that explains social change and stability as a process of negotiated exchanges between parties. Social _____ posits that all human relationships are formed by the use of a subjective cost-benefit analysis and the comparison of alternatives. For example, when a person perceives the costs of a relationship as outweighing the perceived benefits, then the theory predicts that the person will choose to leave the relationship.
   a. A Stake in the Outcome
   b. A4e
   c. AAAI
   d. Exchange theory

20. _____ describes how content an individual is with his or her job.

The happier people are within their job, the more satisfied they are said to be. _____ is not the same as motivation, although it is clearly linked.

   a. Graduate recruitment
   b. Life Orientations Training
   c. Resource dependence
   d. Job satisfaction

21. Leadership is one of the primary areas of study, research, and practice in organizational behavior. Leaders often develop relationships with each member of the group that they lead, and _____ explains how those relationships with various members can develop in unique ways.

The _____ of leadership focuses on the two-way relationship between supervisors and subordinates.

   a. Groups decision making
   b. Human Centered Systems
   c. Light curtains
   d. Leader-Member Exchange theory

22. _____ is the set of reasons that determines one to engage in a particular behavior. The term is generally used for human _____ but, theoretically, it can be used to describe the causes for animal behavior as well
   a. Motivation
   b. Work behavior
   c. Losada Zone
   d. Losada line

23. _____ is a set of properties of the work environment, perceived directly or indirectly by employees, that is assumed to be a major force in influencing employee behavior. (Organizational Behavior ' Management, 8th Ed., Ivancevich, Konopaske, and Matteson)

A Queensland University of Technology view on _____...

The concept of _____ has been assessed by various authors, of which many of them published their own definition of organisational climate.

   a. Abraham Harold Maslow
   b. Organizational climate
   c. Adam Smith
   d. Affiliation

24. In probability theory and statistics, _____ indicates the strength and direction of a linear relationship between two random variables. That is in contrast with the usage of the term in colloquial speech, denoting any relationship, not necessarily linear. In general statistical usage, _____ or co-relation refers to the departure of two random variables from independence.
   a. Correlation
   b. Standard deviation
   c. Statistics
   d. Meta-analysis

25. The sociologist Max Weber defined _____ as 'resting on devotion to the exceptional sanctity, heroism or exemplary character of an individual person, and of the normative patterns or order revealed or ordained by him.' _____ is one of three forms of authority laid out in Weber's tripartite classification of authority, the other two being traditional authority and rational-legal authority. The concept has acquired wide usage among sociologists.

In his writings about _____, Weber applies the term charisma to 'a certain quality of an individual personality, by virtue of which he is set apart from ordinary men and treated as endowed with supernatural, superhuman, or at least specifically exceptional powers or qualities.

   a. Charismatic authority
   b. 33 Strategies of War
   c. 28-hour day
   d. 1990 Clean Air Act

Chapter 4. Assessing Leadership and Measuring Its Effects

26. The terms '_____' and 'independent variable' are used in similar but subtly different ways in mathematics and statistics as part of the standard terminology in those subjects. They are used to distinguish between two types of quantities being considered, separating them into those available at the start of a process and those being created by it, where the latter (_____s) are dependent on the former (independent variables.)

In traditional calculus, a function is defined as a relation between two terms called variables because their values vary.

a. 33 Strategies of War
b. 1990 Clean Air Act
c. 28-hour day
d. Dependent variable

27. In psychology, the 'Big Five' personality traits are five broad factors or dimensions of personality developed through lexical analysis. This is the rational and statistical analysis of words related to personality as found in natural-language dictionaries. The traits are also referred to as the '_____'.
a. Groupthink
b. Conformity
c. Behaviorism
d. Five Factor Model

28. _____ is a term used to classify a group leadership theories that inquire the interactions between leaders and followers. A transactional leader focuses more on a series of 'transactions'. This person is interested in looking out for oneself, having exchange benefits with their subordinates and clarify a sense of duty with rewards and punishments to reach goals.
a. Transactional leadership
b. Reflective listening
c. Care perspective
d. Negative affectivity

29. The _____ is a leadership theory in the field of organizational studies developed by Robert House in 1971 and revised in 1996. The theory that a leader's behavior is contingent to the satisfaction, motivation and performance of subordinates. The revised version also argues that the leader engage in behaviors that complement subordinate's abilities and compensate for deficiencies.
a. Job analysis
b. Leadership development
c. Work design
d. Path-goal theory

Chapter 4. Assessing Leadership and Measuring Its Effects

30. More recently organizations have come to understand that leadership can also be developed by strengthening the connection between and alignment of the efforts of individual leaders and the systems through which they influence organizational operations. This has led to a differentiation between leader development and _____. Leader development focuses on the development of the leader, such as the personal attributes desired in a leader, desired ways of behaving, ways of thinking or feeling.
    a. Pseudoconsensus
    b. Path-goal theory
    c. Group process consultation
    d. Leadership development

31. _____ is purposeful and reflective judgment about what to believe or what to do in response to observations, experience, verbal or written expressions, or arguments. _____ might involve determining the meaning and significance of what is observed or expressed, or, concerning a given inference or argument, determining whether there is adequate justification to accept the conclusion as true. Hence, Fisher ' Scriven define _____ as 'Skilled, active, interpretation and evaluation of observations, communications, information, and argumentation.' Parker ' Moore define it more narrowly as the careful, deliberate determination of whether one should accept, reject, or suspend judgment about a claim and the degree of confidence with which one accepts or rejects it.
    a. 1990 Clean Air Act
    b. Critical thinking
    c. Virtual team
    d. Succession planning

Chapter 5. Power and Influence

1. _____ or just peck order is a hierarchical system of social organization in animals. It was first described from the behaviour of poultry by Thorleif Schjelderup-Ebbe in 1921 under the German terms Hackordnung or Hackliste and introduced into English in 1925. The original usage of 'peck order' referred to expression of dominance of birds.
    a. Sexual sublimation
    b. Bandwagon effect
    c. Human rights
    d. Pecking order

2. The sociologist Max Weber defined _____ as 'resting on devotion to the exceptional sanctity, heroism or exemplary character of an individual person, and of the normative patterns or order revealed or ordained by him.' _____ is one of three forms of authority laid out in Weber's tripartite classification of authority, the other two being traditional authority and rational-legal authority. The concept has acquired wide usage among sociologists.

    In his writings about _____, Weber applies the term charisma to 'a certain quality of an individual personality, by virtue of which he is set apart from ordinary men and treated as endowed with supernatural, superhuman, or at least specifically exceptional powers or qualities.

    a. 1990 Clean Air Act
    b. 28-hour day
    c. 33 Strategies of War
    d. Charismatic authority

3. _____ is a leadership style that defines as leadership that creates voluble and positive change in the followers. A transformational leader focuses on 'transforming' others to help each other, to look out for each other, be encouraging, harmonious, and look out for the organization as a whole. In this leadership, the leader enhances the motivation, moral and performance of his follower group.
    a. Subpersonality
    b. Need for affiliation
    c. Milgram experiment
    d. Transformational leadership

4. Social _____ is a social psychological and sociological perspective that explains social change and stability as a process of negotiated exchanges between parties. Social _____ posits that all human relationships are formed by the use of a subjective cost-benefit analysis and the comparison of alternatives. For example, when a person perceives the costs of a relationship as outweighing the perceived benefits, then the theory predicts that the person will choose to leave the relationship.

a. AAAI
b. A Stake in the Outcome
c. A4e
d. Exchange theory

5. Leadership is one of the primary areas of study, research, and practice in organizational behavior. Leaders often develop relationships with each member of the group that they lead, and _____ explains how those relationships with various members can develop in unique ways.

The _____ of leadership focuses on the two-way relationship between supervisors and subordinates.

a. Human Centered Systems
b. Light curtains
c. Groups decision making
d. Leader-Member Exchange theory

6. The _____ was a study of the psychological effects of becoming a prisoner or prison guard. The experiment was conducted in 1971 by a team of researchers led by Psychology Professor Philip Zimbardo at Stanford University. Twenty-four undergraduates were selected out of 70 to play the roles of both guards and prisoners and live in a mock prison in the basement of the Stanford psychology building. Those selected were chosen for their lack of psychological issues, crime history, and medical disabilities, in order to obtain a representative sample. Roles were assigned based on a coin toss.

Prisoners and guards rapidly adapted to their roles, stepping beyond the boundaries of what had been predicted and leading to dangerous and psychologically damaging situations. One-third of the guards were judged to have exhibited 'genuine' sadistic tendencies, while many prisoners were emotionally traumatized and two had to be removed from the experiment early.

a. Stanford Prison experiment
b. 28-hour day
c. 33 Strategies of War
d. 1990 Clean Air Act

7. _____ is individual power based on a high level of identification with, admiration of, or respect for the powerholder.

Nationalism, Patriotism, Celebrities and well-respected people are examples of _____ in effect.

_____ is one of the Five Bases of Social Power, as defined by Bertram Raven and his colleagues[1] in 1959.

a. Transfer of training
b. Reflective listening
c. Convergent thinking
d. Referent power

8. _____ is the practice of compelling a person or manipulating them to behave in an involuntary way by use of threats, intimidation, trickery, or some other form of pressure or force. These are used as leverage, to force the victim to act in the desired way. _____ may involve the actual infliction of physical pain/injury or psychological harm in order to enhance the credibility of a threat.
    a. Coercion
    b. 28-hour day
    c. Good faith
    d. 1990 Clean Air Act

9. _____ refers to increasing the spiritual, political, social or economic strength of individuals and communities. It often involves the empowered developing confidence in their own capacities.

The term Human _____ covers a vast landscape of meanings, interpretations, definitions and disciplines ranging from psychology and philosophy to the highly commercialized Self-Help industry and Motivational sciences.

    a. Empowerment
    b. Institutionalisation
    c. Emotional labor
    d. Institutionalization

10. _____ is a term used to classify a group leadership theories that inquire the interactions between leaders and followers. A transactional leader focuses more on a series of 'transactions'. This person is interested in looking out for oneself, having exchange benefits with their subordinates and clarify a sense of duty with rewards and punishments to reach goals.
    a. Reflective listening
    b. Transactional leadership
    c. Care perspective
    d. Negative affectivity

11. _____ is a term that was popularized by renowned psychologist David McClelland in 1961. However, it should be recognized that McClellend's thinking was strongly influenced by the pioneering work of Henry Murray who first identified underlying psychological human needs and motivational processes (1938.) It was Murray who set out a taxonomy of needs, including Achievement, Power and Affiliation - and placed these in the context of an integrated motivational model.
   a. Mortality salience
   b. Two-factor theory
   c. Need for power
   d. Holland Codes

12. A _____ aims to describe aspects of a person's character that remain stable throughout that person's lifetime, the individual's character pattern of behavior, thoughts, and feelings. An early model of personality was posited by Greek philosopher/physician Hippocrates. The 20th century heralded a new interest in defining and identifying separate personality types, in close correlation with the emergence of the field of psychology.
   a. Taylor-Johnson Temperament Analysis
   b. Picture Arrangement Test
   c. Morrisby Profile
   d. Personality test

13. _____ is the set of reasons that determines one to engage in a particular behavior. The term is generally used for human _____ but, theoretically, it can be used to describe the causes for animal behavior as well
   a. Work behavior
   b. Losada Zone
   c. Motivation
   d. Losada line

14. '_____ is a strategic attempt to get someone to like you in order to obtain compliance with a request (Vaughan, ' Hogg, 2008.) _____ is generally conceptualized as a variant of impression management tactics (Buss, Gomes, Higgins ' Lauterbach, 1987.)

Chapter 5. Power and Influence

According to Jones (Eugene, 1966), the three major tactics for _____ are other-enhancement, opinion conformity, and self-presentation.

- Other-enhancement means flattery. People use this tactic to gain compliance by flattering an individual or reasoning with him or her instead of forcing compliance. The person focuses and often exaggerates the positive side, and ignores the negative side, with the goal to communicate the idea that the ingratiator thinks highly of the other person. This tactic succeeds often because people find it difficult not to like people who think highly of them. Basically, the ingratiatory wants to be liked by showing liking and modesty, making himself/herself physically attractive and generating similarity towards the target person.
- Opinion conformity is conforming to the various ways of the target person. The belief is that people like those with apparently similar values. Allow the target to 'convince' you of their opinion. Either consistent conformity or conformity preceded by sufficient resistance are both good strategies at _____.
- Self-presentation is to present one's own attributes in a manner that the target would approve and like. The level of status between the ingratiator and target are important. 'Relatively high status individuals were more modest when induced to become ingratiating, while relatively low status individuals were more self-enhancing but only in predictable respects' (Eugene, 1966.)

a. Ingratiation
b. AAAI
c. A Stake in the Outcome
d. A4e

15. A _____ is a distinction of biological and/or physiological characteristics typically associated with either males or females of a species in general. In the study of humans, socio-political issues arise in classifying whether a sex difference results from the biology of gender
    a. Gender difference
    b. Mediation
    c. Living wage
    d. McJob

16. _____ is the name applied to two competing management theories. One was developed by Abraham H. Maslow in his book Maslow on Management and the other is Dr. William Ouchi's so-called 'Japanese Management' style popularized during the Asian economic boom of the 1980s. In contrast Theory X, which stated that workers inherently dislike and avoid work and must be driven to it, and Theory Y, which stated that work is natural and can be a source of satisfaction when aimed at higher order human psychological needs, _____ focused on increasing employee loyalty to the company by providing a job for life with a strong focus on the well-being of the employee, both on and off the job.

a. 33 Strategies of War
b. 1990 Clean Air Act
c. 28-hour day
d. Theory Z

Chapter 6. Leadership and Values

1. The sociologist Max Weber defined _____ as 'resting on devotion to the exceptional sanctity, heroism or exemplary character of an individual person, and of the normative patterns or order revealed or ordained by him.' _____ is one of three forms of authority laid out in Weber's tripartite classification of authority, the other two being traditional authority and rational-legal authority. The concept has acquired wide usage among sociologists.

   In his writings about _____, Weber applies the term charisma to 'a certain quality of an individual personality, by virtue of which he is set apart from ordinary men and treated as endowed with supernatural, superhuman, or at least specifically exceptional powers or qualities.

   a. Charismatic authority
   b. 33 Strategies of War
   c. 1990 Clean Air Act
   d. 28-hour day

2. _____ are theories of human motivation created and developed by Douglas McGregor at the MIT Sloan School of Management in the 1960s that have been used in human resource management, organizational behavior, organizational communication and organizational development. They describe two very different attitudes toward workforce motivation. McGregor felt that companies followed either one or the other approach.

   The first approach which many managers practice, management assumes employees are inherently lazy and will avoid work if they can. They inherently dislike work. Because of this, workers need to be closely supervised and comprehensive systems of controls developed.

   In the second approach, management assumes employees may be ambitious and self-motivated and exercise self-control. It is believed that employees enjoy their mental and physical work duties.

   a. Resource-based view
   b. Management by exception
   c. Theory X and theory Y
   d. Senior management

3. _____ is a term used to classify a group leadership theories that inquire the interactions between leaders and followers. A transactional leader focuses more on a series of 'transactions'. This person is interested in looking out for oneself, having exchange benefits with their subordinates and clarify a sense of duty with rewards and punishments to reach goals.
   a. Care perspective
   b. Transactional leadership
   c. Reflective listening
   d. Negative affectivity

Chapter 6. Leadership and Values 31

4. _____ is a leadership style that defines as leadership that creates voluble and positive change in the followers. A transformational leader focuses on 'transforming' others to help each other, to look out for each other, be encouraging, harmonious, and look out for the organization as a whole. In this leadership, the leader enhances the motivation, moral and performance of his follower group.

   a. Subpersonality
   b. Milgram experiment
   c. Need for affiliation
   d. Transformational leadership

5. _____ is the value of objects, both physical objects and abstract objects, not as ends-in-themselves but a means of achieving something else. It is often contrasted with items of intrinsic value.

It is studied in the field of value theory.

   a. A4e
   b. A Stake in the Outcome
   c. Instrumental value
   d. AAAI

6. _____ is a term which portrays a generation born during the middle part of the 20th Century. The birth years of the _____ are the subject of controversy. Historically, everyone born during the post-World War II demographic boom in births was called part of the _____.

   a. Wal-Mart
   b. Baby Boom Generation
   c. Adam Smith
   d. Abraham Harold Maslow

7. _____ is the identity of a group or culture, or of an individual as far as one is influenced by one's belonging to a group or culture. _____ is similar to and has overlaps with, but is not synonymous with, identity politics.

There are modern questions of culture that are transferred into questions of identity.

   a. Cultural identity
   b. Functionalism
   c. 1990 Clean Air Act
   d. 28-hour day

Chapter 6. Leadership and Values

8. A _____ is a research instrument consisting of a series of questions and other prompts for the purpose of gathering information from respondents. Although they are often designed for statistical analysis of the responses, this is not always the case. The _____ was invented by Sir Francis Galton.
   a. Questionnaire
   b. 28-hour day
   c. Structured interview
   d. 1990 Clean Air Act

9. The _____ was a study of the psychological effects of becoming a prisoner or prison guard. The experiment was conducted in 1971 by a team of researchers led by Psychology Professor Philip Zimbardo at Stanford University. Twenty-four undergraduates were selected out of 70 to play the roles of both guards and prisoners and live in a mock prison in the basement of the Stanford psychology building. Those selected were chosen for their lack of psychological issues, crime history, and medical disabilities, in order to obtain a representative sample. Roles were assigned based on a coin toss.

Prisoners and guards rapidly adapted to their roles, stepping beyond the boundaries of what had been predicted and leading to dangerous and psychologically damaging situations. One-third of the guards were judged to have exhibited 'genuine' sadistic tendencies, while many prisoners were emotionally traumatized and two had to be removed from the experiment early.

   a. 33 Strategies of War
   b. 1990 Clean Air Act
   c. Stanford Prison experiment
   d. 28-hour day

10. _____ is a school of philosophy which argues that pleasure has an ultimate importance and is the most important pursuit of humanity.

The name derives from the Greek word for 'delight'.

The basic idea behind hedonistic thought is that pleasure is the only thing that is good for a person; indeed: the only good.

   a. 1990 Clean Air Act
   b. Determinism
   c. 28-hour day
   d. Hedonism

Chapter 6. Leadership and Values 33

11. _____ is the name applied to two competing management theories. One was developed by Abraham H. Maslow in his book Maslow on Management and the other is Dr. William Ouchi's so-called 'Japanese Management' style popularized during the Asian economic boom of the 1980s. In contrast Theory X, which stated that workers inherently dislike and avoid work and must be driven to it, and Theory Y, which stated that work is natural and can be a source of satisfaction when aimed at higher order human psychological needs, _____ focused on increasing employee loyalty to the company by providing a job for life with a strong focus on the well-being of the employee, both on and off the job.
  a. Theory Z
  b. 1990 Clean Air Act
  c. 33 Strategies of War
  d. 28-hour day

12. _____ is an idea in the field of Organizational studies and management which describes the psychology, attitudes, experiences, beliefs and Values (personal and cultural values) of an organization. It has been defined as 'the specific collection of values and norms that are shared by people and groups in an organization and that control the way they interact with each other and with stakeholders outside the organization.'

This definition continues to explain organizational values also known as 'beliefs and ideas about what kinds of goals members of an organization should pursue and ideas about the appropriate kinds or standards of behavior organizational members should use to achieve these goals. From organizational values develop organizational norms, guidelines or expectations that prescribe appropriate kinds of behavior by employees in particular situations and control the behavior of organizational members towards one another.'

_____ is not the same as corporate culture.

  a. A Stake in the Outcome
  b. AAAI
  c. A4e
  d. Organizational culture

13. _____ is a method of directing, instructing and training a person or group of people, with the aim to achieve some goal or develop specific skills. There are many ways to coach, types of _____ and methods to _____. Direction may include motivational speaking.
  a. Co-coaching
  b. 1990 Clean Air Act
  c. 28-hour day
  d. Coaching

14. _____ is the imitation of some real thing, state of affairs, or process. The act of simulating something generally entails representing certain key characteristics or behaviours of a selected physical or abstract system.

Chapter 6. Leadership and Values

_____ is used in many contexts, including the modeling of natural systems or human systems in order to gain insight into their functioning.

a. 28-hour day
b. Simulation
c. 33 Strategies of War
d. 1990 Clean Air Act

15. The _____ captures an expanded spectrum of values and criteria for measuring organizational success: economic, ecological and social. With the ratification of the United Nations and ICLEI _____ standard for urban and community accounting in early 2007, this became the dominant approach to public sector full cost accounting. Similar UN standards apply to natural capital and human capital measurement to assist in measurements required by _____, e.g. the ecoBudget standard for reporting ecological footprint.

a. 33 Strategies of War
b. 28-hour day
c. 1990 Clean Air Act
d. Triple bottom line

16. In the arts and antiques, _____ is the judgment by experts as to the authorship, date, or other aspect of the origin of a work of art or cultural artifact. Works 'attributed' to an artist are more firmly believed to be theirs than those 'ascribed'.

_____ can also mean:

- _____, a concept in copyright law requiring an author to be credited
- Journalism sourcing (or _____), a journalistic practice of attributing information to its source
- _____ (psychology), a concept in psychology whereby people attribute traits and causes to things they observe
- Performance _____, a technique in quantitative finance for explaining the active performance of a portfolio

a. A4e
b. A Stake in the Outcome
c. Ambition
d. Attribution

Chapter 6. Leadership and Values

17. _____ is the process by which members of a group of people assert the 'inferiority' of another group through subtle or overt acts or statements. _____ may be directed by an organization (such as a state) or may be the composite of individual sentiments and actions, as with some types of de facto racism. State-organized _____ has been directed against perceived racial or ethnic groups, nationalities (or 'foreigners' in general), religious groups, genders, minorities of various sexual orientations (eg.
    a. Dehumanization
    b. Role model
    c. Spheres of influence
    d. Role conflict

18. _____ is a social phenomenon which tends to occur in groups of people above a certain critical size when responsibility is not explicitly assigned. This mindset can be seen in the phrase 'No one raindrop thinks it caused the flood'.

    _____ can manifest itself:

    - in a group of people who, through action or inaction, allow events to occur which they would never allow if they were alone. Examples include groupthink and the bystander effect.
    - in a group of people working on a task that loses motivation because people feel less responsible and hide their lack of effort in the group (social loafing.)
    - in hierarchical organizations, such as when underlings claim that they were just following orders and supervisors claim that they were just issuing directives and not doing the deeds.

    a. Groupthink
    b. Cognitive dissonance
    c. Psychological testing
    d. Diffusion of responsibility

19. Organizational culture is not the same as _____. It is wider and deeper concepts, something that an organization 'is' rather than what it 'has' (according to Buchanan and Huczynski.)

    _____ is the total sum of the values, customs, traditions and meanings that make a company unique.

    a. Graduate recruitment
    b. Cross-functional team
    c. Merit Shop
    d. Corporate culture

Chapter 6. Leadership and Values

20. _____ is a concept in ethics with several meanings. It is often used synonymously with such concepts as responsibility, answerability, enforcement, blameworthiness, liability and other terms associated with the expectation of account-giving. As an aspect of governance, it has been central to discussions related to problems in both the public and private (corporation) worlds.

a. A Stake in the Outcome
b. A4e
c. AAAI
d. Accountability

21. An _____ is a form of government in which the political power is held by a single, self-appointed ruler. The term autocrat is derived from the Greek word 'αυτοκρῐ́τωρ. Compare with oligarchy ('rule by the few') and democracy ('rule by the people'.)

a. A Stake in the Outcome
b. Autocracy
c. AAAI
d. A4e

22. In economics, the term _____ refers to situations where the advancement of a qualified person within the hierarchy of an organization is stopped at a lower level because of some form of discrimination, most commonly sexism or racism, but since the term was coined, '_____' has also come to describe the limited advancement of the deaf, blind, disabled, aged and sexual minorities. It is an unofficial, invisible barrier that prevents women and minorities from advancing in businesses.

This situation is referred to as a 'ceiling' as there is a limitation blocking upward advancement, and 'glass' (transparent) because the limitation is not immediately apparent and is normally an unwritten and unofficial policy. This invisible barrier continues to exist, even though there are no explicit obstacles keeping minorities from acquiring advanced job positions - there are no advertisements that specifically say 'no minorities hired at this establishment', nor are there any formal orders that say 'minorities are not qualified' - but they do lie beneath the surface.

a. 1990 Clean Air Act
b. 33 Strategies of War
c. 28-hour day
d. Glass ceiling

Chapter 7. Leadership Traits

1. _____ is a class of behavioural theory that claims that there is no best way to organize a corporation, to lead a company, or to make decisions. Instead, the optimal course of action is contingent (dependant) upon the internal and external situation. Several contingency approaches were developed concurrently in the late 1960s.
   a. Senior management
   b. Contingency Theory
   c. Goal setting
   d. Resource-based view

2. In psychology, _____ is a major approach to the study of human personality. Trait theorists are primarily interested in the measurement of traits, which can be defined as habitual patterns of behavior, thought, and emotion. According to this perspective, traits are relatively stable over time, differ among individuals (e.g. some people are outgoing whereas others are shy), and influence behavior.
   a. Groupthink
   b. Beck Depression Inventory
   c. Positive psychology
   d. Trait theory

3. In psychology, the 'Big Five' personality traits are five broad factors or dimensions of personality developed through lexical analysis. This is the rational and statistical analysis of words related to personality as found in natural-language dictionaries. The traits are also referred to as the '_____'.
   a. Groupthink
   b. Conformity
   c. Behaviorism
   d. Five Factor Model

4. _____ is a personality attribute that is part of the Big Five personality traits, or the Five-factor model (FFM.) It is most commonly referred to as the dimension of Extraversion. Though nowadays is referred to as a self-reported construct, it was associated by Cattell (1947, 1948) also to an ability, namely the word fluency ability identified by Thurstone and Thurstone (1941.)
   a. 1990 Clean Air Act
   b. Surgency
   c. 28-hour day
   d. 33 Strategies of War

5. _____ is a tendency to be pleasant and accommodating in social situations. In contemporary personality psychology, _____ is one of the five major dimensions of personality structure, reflecting individual differences in concern for cooperation and social harmony. People who score high on this dimension are on average more empathetic, considerate, friendly, generous, and helpful.

Chapter 7. Leadership Traits

a. A Stake in the Outcome
b. A4e
c. Extraversion
d. Agreeableness

6. _____ is one of five major domains of personality discovered by psychologists. Openness involves active imagination, aesthetic sensitivity, attentiveness to inner feelings, preference for variety, and intellectual curiosity. A great deal of psychometric research has demonstrated that these qualities are statistically correlated.
   a. Extraversion
   b. A4e
   c. Openness to experience
   d. A Stake in the Outcome

7. _____ is the possession of motivation for power. Ambitious persons seek power either for themselves or for others. People can wield their acquired power in the name of a vague or clear ideal or multiple ideals.
   a. A4e
   b. Attribution
   c. A Stake in the Outcome
   d. Ambition

8. _____ Stores, Inc. is an American public corporation that runs a chain of large, discount department stores. It is the world's largest public corporation by revenue, according to the 2008 Fortune Global 500.
   a. Adam Smith
   b. Wal-Mart
   c. William Edwards Deming
   d. Abraham Harold Maslow

9. The trait of _____ is a central dimension of human personality. Extraverts (also spelled extroverts) tend to be gregarious, assertive, and interested in seeking out excitement. Introverts, in contrast, tend to be more reserved, less outgoing, and less sociable.

Chapter 7. Leadership Traits

a. Extraversion
b. Extraversion-introversion
c. A Stake in the Outcome
d. Openness to experience

10. A _____ aims to describe aspects of a person's character that remain stable throughout that person's lifetime, the individual's character pattern of behavior, thoughts, and feelings. An early model of personality was posited by Greek philosopher/physician Hippocrates. The 20th century heralded a new interest in defining and identifying separate personality types, in close correlation with the emergence of the field of psychology.

a. Taylor-Johnson Temperament Analysis
b. Morrisby Profile
c. Picture Arrangement Test
d. Personality test

11. The concept of _____ refers to the psychological classification of different types of individuals. _____s can be distinguished from personality traits, which come in different levels or degrees. Types involve qualitative differences between people, whereas traits involve quantitative differences.

a. 33 Strategies of War
b. 1990 Clean Air Act
c. 28-hour day
d. Personality type

12. _____ is an idea in the field of Organizational studies and management which describes the psychology, attitudes, experiences, beliefs and Values (personal and cultural values) of an organization. It has been defined as 'the specific collection of values and norms that are shared by people and groups in an organization and that control the way they interact with each other and with stakeholders outside the organization.'

This definition continues to explain organizational values also known as 'beliefs and ideas about what kinds of goals members of an organization should pursue and ideas about the appropriate kinds or standards of behavior organizational members should use to achieve these goals. From organizational values develop organizational norms, guidelines or expectations that prescribe appropriate kinds of behavior by employees in particular situations and control the behavior of organizational members towards one another.'

_____ is not the same as corporate culture.

a. A Stake in the Outcome
b. Organizational culture
c. AAAI
d. A4e

13. _____ is a method of directing, instructing and training a person or group of people, with the aim to achieve some goal or develop specific skills. There are many ways to coach, types of _____ and methods to _____. Direction may include motivational speaking.
   a. 28-hour day
   b. 1990 Clean Air Act
   c. Co-coaching
   d. Coaching

14. The _____ of Intelligence was formulated by Robert J. Sternberg, a prominent figure in the research of human intelligence. The theory by itself was groundbreaking in that it was among the first to go against the psychometric approach to intelligence and take a more cognitive approach. Sternberge;s definition of human intelligence is e;(a) mental activity directed toward purposive adaptation to, selection and shaping of, real-world environments relevant to onee;s lifee; (Sternberg, 1985, p.
   a. Triarchic theory of intelligence
   b. Triarchic theory
   c. Learning theories
   d. Goal theory

15. The _____ was formulated by Robert J. Sternberg, a prominent figure in the research of human intelligence. The theory by itself was groundbreaking in that it was among the first to go against the psychometric approach to intelligence and take a more cognitive approach. Sternberge;s definition of human intelligence is e;(a) mental activity directed toward purposive adaptation to, selection and shaping of, real-world environments relevant to onee;s lifee; (Sternberg, 1985, p.
   a. Peer support
   b. Programmed instruction
   c. Learning theories
   d. Triarchic theory of intelligence

16. _____ is the set of reasons that determines one to engage in a particular behavior. The term is generally used for human _____ but, theoretically, it can be used to describe the causes for animal behavior as well

a. Motivation
b. Work behavior
c. Losada Zone
d. Losada line

17. _____ is a term coined by Joy Paul Guilford as the opposite of divergent thinking. It generally means the ability to give the correct answer to standard questions that do not require significant creativity, for instance in most tasks in school and on standardized multiple-choice tests for intelligence.
    a. Differential item functioning
    b. Convergent thinking
    c. Care perspective
    d. Negative affectivity

18. _____ is a thought process or method, which is usually applied with the goal to generate ideas. It is often used for creative and problem solving purposes in conjunction with Convergent thinking. There are different methods in _____.
    a. Functional fixedness
    b. 1990 Clean Air Act
    c. Divergent thinking
    d. Problem solving

19. _____ is the state achieved by coming together, the state of agreement. The Latin congruere means to come together, agree. As an abstract term, _____ means similarity between objects.
    a. Turnover
    b. HMIS
    c. The Goodyear Tire ' Rubber Company
    d. Congruence

20. In epidemiology, _____ are those determinants of disease that are not transmitted genetically. Apart from the true monogenic genetic disorders, _____ may determine the development of disease in those genetically predisposed to a particular condition. Stress, physical and mental abuse, Diet, exposure to toxins, pathogens, radiation and chemicals found in almost all personal care products and household cleaners are common _____ that determine a large segment of non-hereditary disease.

a. A Stake in the Outcome
b. A4e
c. AAAI
d. Environmental factors

21. The term _____ denotes a property of some thing or action which is essential and specific to that thing or action, and which is wholly independent of any other object, action or consequence. A characteristic which is not essential or inherent is extrinsic.

For example in biology, _____ effects originate from 'inside' an organism or cell, such as an autoimmune disease or _____ immunity.

a. A Stake in the Outcome
b. AAAI
c. A4e
d. Intrinsic

22. _____ comes from rewards inherent to a task or activity itself - the enjoyment of a puzzle or the love of playing basketball, for example. One is said to be intrinsically motivated when engaging in an activity 'with no apparent reward except for the activity itself'. This form of motivation has been studied by social and educational psychologists since the early 1970s.
a. A4e
b. Extrinsic motivation
c. A Stake in the Outcome
d. Intrinsic motivation

23. Cognition is the scientific term for 'the process of thought'. Its usage varies in different ways in accord with different disciplines: For example, in psychology and _____ science it refers to an information processing view of an individual's psychological functions. Other interpretations of the meaning of cognition link it to the development of concepts; individual minds, groups, organizations, and even larger coalitions of entities, can be modelled as 'societies' (Society of Mind), which cooperate to form concepts.
a. Disabilities
b. Cognitive processes
c. Generation Y
d. Cognitive

24. _____--which is related to creeping featurism and second-system effect--is the tendency of programmers to disproportionately emphasize elegance in software at the expense of other requirements such as functionality, shipping schedule, and usability.

a. 28-hour day
b. 1990 Clean Air Act
c. 33 Strategies of War
d. Creeping elegance

25. _____ , often measured as an _____ Quotient (EQ), is a term that describes the ability, capacity, skill or (in the case of the trait _____ model) a self-perceived ability, to identify, assess, and manage the emotions of one's self, of others, and of groups. Different models have been proposed for the definition of _____ and disagreement exists as to how the term should be used. Despite these disagreements, which are often highly technical, the ability _____ and trait _____ models (but not the mixed models) are enjoying considerable support in the literature and have successful applications in many different domains.
   a. A4e
   b. Emotional exhaustion
   c. Emotional intelligence
   d. A Stake in the Outcome

Chapter 8. Leadership Behavior

1. _____ psychology focuses on this second level of study. It is also sometimes called Differential Psychology because researchers in this area study the ways in which individual people differ in their behavior. This is distinguished from other aspects of psychology in that although psychology is ostensibly a study of individuals, modern psychologists often study groups or biological underpinnings of cognition.

   a. Expectancy
   b. Expectancy theory
   c. A Stake in the Outcome
   d. Individual differences

2. In human resources or industrial/organizational psychology, _____' 'multisource feedback,' or 'multisource assessment,' is feedback that comes from all around an employee. '360' refers to the 360 degrees in a circle, with an individual figuratively in the center of the circle. Feedback is provided by subordinates, peers, and supervisors.

   a. Human resources
   b. ROWE
   c. Professional in Human Resources
   d. 360-degree feedback

3. _____ describes the situation when output from (or information about the result of) an event or phenomenon in the past will influence the same event/phenomenon in the present or future. When an event is part of a chain of cause-and-effect that forms a circuit or loop, then the event is said to 'feed back' into itself.

   _____ is also a synonym for:

   - _____ Signal; the information about the initial event that is the basis for subsequent modification of the event.
   - _____ Loop; the causal path that leads from the initial generation of the _____ signal to the subsequent modification of the event.

   _____ is a mechanism, process or signal that is looped back to control a system within itself. Such a loop is called a _____ loop.

   a. 28-hour day
   b. 1990 Clean Air Act
   c. Positive feedback
   d. Feedback

4. A _____ is the learned capacity to carry out pre-determined results often with the minimum outlay of time, energy, or both. _____s can often be divided into domain-general and domain-specific _____s. For example, in the domain of work, some general _____s would include time management, teamwork and leadership, self motivation and others, whereas domain-specific _____s would be useful only for a certain job.

a. 1990 Clean Air Act
b. 28-hour day
c. 33 Strategies of War
d. Skill

5. A _____ is a research instrument consisting of a series of questions and other prompts for the purpose of gathering information from respondents. Although they are often designed for statistical analysis of the responses, this is not always the case. The _____ was invented by Sir Francis Galton.
   a. 1990 Clean Air Act
   b. Structured interview
   c. Questionnaire
   d. 28-hour day

6. A _____ or objective is a projected state of affairs that a person or a system plans or intends to achieve--a personal or organizational desired end-point in some sort of assumed development. Many people endeavor to reach _____s within a finite time by setting deadlines.

A desire or an intention becomes a _____ if and only if one activates an action for achieving it

   a. Goal
   b. Span of control
   c. Task list
   d. Management by exception

7. _____ is a kind of action that occurs as two or more objects have an effect upon one another. The idea of a two-way effect is essential in the concept of _____, as opposed to a one-way causal effect. A closely related term is interconnectivity, which deals with the _____s of _____s within systems: combinations of many simple _____s can lead to surprising emergent phenomena.
   a. Organizational communication
   b. Interpersonal communication
   c. Organizational dissent
   d. Interaction

8. The _____ captures an expanded spectrum of values and criteria for measuring organizational success: economic, ecological and social. With the ratification of the United Nations and ICLEI _____ standard for urban and community accounting in early 2007, this became the dominant approach to public sector full cost accounting. Similar UN standards apply to natural capital and human capital measurement to assist in measurements required by _____, e.g. the ecoBudget standard for reporting ecological footprint.

a. 28-hour day
b. Triple bottom line
c. 33 Strategies of War
d. 1990 Clean Air Act

9. The sociologist Max Weber defined _____ as 'resting on devotion to the exceptional sanctity, heroism or exemplary character of an individual person, and of the normative patterns or order revealed or ordained by him.' _____ is one of three forms of authority laid out in Weber's tripartite classification of authority, the other two being traditional authority and rational-legal authority. The concept has acquired wide usage among sociologists.

In his writings about _____, Weber applies the term charisma to 'a certain quality of an individual personality, by virtue of which he is set apart from ordinary men and treated as endowed with supernatural, superhuman, or at least specifically exceptional powers or qualities.

a. 28-hour day
b. 33 Strategies of War
c. 1990 Clean Air Act
d. Charismatic authority

10. In economics, the term _____ refers to situations where the advancement of a qualified person within the hierarchy of an organization is stopped at a lower level because of some form of discrimination, most commonly sexism or racism, but since the term was coined, '_____' has also come to describe the limited advancement of the deaf, blind, disabled, aged and sexual minorities. It is an unofficial, invisible barrier that prevents women and minorities from advancing in businesses.

This situation is referred to as a 'ceiling' as there is a limitation blocking upward advancement, and 'glass' (transparent) because the limitation is not immediately apparent and is normally an unwritten and unofficial policy. This invisible barrier continues to exist, even though there are no explicit obstacles keeping minorities from acquiring advanced job positions - there are no advertisements that specifically say 'no minorities hired at this establishment', nor are there any formal orders that say 'minorities are not qualified' - but they do lie beneath the surface.

a. 33 Strategies of War
b. 28-hour day
c. 1990 Clean Air Act
d. Glass ceiling

Chapter 8. Leadership Behavior

11. A _____ is a member of a species of bipedal primates in the family Hominidae. DNA and fossil evidence indicates that modern _____s originated in east Africa about 200,000 years ago. When compared to other animals and primates, _____s have a highly developed brain, capable of abstract reasoning, language, introspection and problem solving.
   a. Side letter
   b. Human
   c. Sourcing
   d. Fast track negotiating authority

12. _____ is a joint action by two or more people or a group, in which each person contributes with different skills and Express his or her individual interests and opinions to the unity and efficiency of the group in order to achieve common goals.

This does not mean that the individual is no longer important; however, it does mean that effective and efficient _____ goes beyond individual accomplishments. The most effective _____ is produced when all the individuals involved harmonize their contributions and work towards a common goal.

   a. 33 Strategies of War
   b. 28-hour day
   c. Teamwork
   d. 1990 Clean Air Act

13. _____ is a term used to classify a group leadership theories that inquire the interactions between leaders and followers. A transactional leader focuses more on a series of 'transactions'. This person is interested in looking out for oneself, having exchange benefits with their subordinates and clarify a sense of duty with rewards and punishments to reach goals.
   a. Negative affectivity
   b. Care perspective
   c. Reflective listening
   d. Transactional leadership

14. _____ is a leadership style that defines as leadership that creates voluble and positive change in the followers. A transformational leader focuses on 'transforming' others to help each other, to look out for each other, be encouraging, harmonious, and look out for the organization as a whole. In this leadership, the leader enhances the motivation, moral and performance of his follower group.
   a. Milgram experiment
   b. Need for affiliation
   c. Transformational leadership
   d. Subpersonality

Chapter 8. Leadership Behavior

15. '_____' refers to mental and communicative algorithms applied during social communications and interactions in order to reach certain effects or results. The term '_____' is used often in business contexts to refer to the measure of a person's ability to operate within business organizations through social communication and interactions. _____ are how people relate to one another.
    a. Intrapersonal communication
    b. A Stake in the Outcome
    c. A4e
    d. Interpersonal skills

16. _____ communication is language use or thought internal to the communicator. _____ communication is the active internal involvement of the individual in symbolic processing of messages. The individual becomes his or her own sender and receiver, providing feedback to him or herself in an ongoing internal process.
    a. A Stake in the Outcome
    b. Intrapersonal
    c. Intrapersonal communication
    d. A4e

17. _____ Stores, Inc. is an American public corporation that runs a chain of large, discount department stores. It is the world's largest public corporation by revenue, according to the 2008 Fortune Global 500.
    a. Adam Smith
    b. Abraham Harold Maslow
    c. William Edwards Deming
    d. Wal-Mart

18. _____ is a social science concept used in business, economics, organizational behaviour, political science, public health and sociology that refers to connections within and between social networks. Though there are a variety of related definitions, which have been described as 'something of a cure-all' for the problems of modern society, they tend to share the core idea 'that social networks have value. Just as a screwdriver (physical capital) or a college education (human capital) can increase productivity (both individual and collective), so do social contacts affect the productivity of individuals and groups'.
    a. Social awareness
    b. Social capital
    c. Spheres of influence
    d. Group cohesiveness

19. _____ is the state achieved by coming together, the state of agreement. The Latin congruere means to come together, agree. As an abstract term, _____ means similarity between objects.

a. The Goodyear Tire ' Rubber Company
b. Turnover
c. HMIS
d. Congruence

20. _____ is a term used to describe a policy of allowing events to take their own course. The term is a French phrase literally meaning 'let do'. It is a doctrine that states that government generally should not intervene in the marketplace.
   a. Laissez-faire
   b. 1990 Clean Air Act
   c. Worker self-management
   d. 28-hour day

21. A _____ is a distinction of biological and/or physiological characteristics typically associated with either males or females of a species in general. In the study of humans, socio-political issues arise in classifying whether a sex difference results from the biology of gender
   a. McJob
   b. Gender difference
   c. Living wage
   d. Mediation

22. _____ is an idea in the field of Organizational studies and management which describes the psychology, attitudes, experiences, beliefs and Values (personal and cultural values) of an organization. It has been defined as 'the specific collection of values and norms that are shared by people and groups in an organization and that control the way they interact with each other and with stakeholders outside the organization.'

This definition continues to explain organizational values also known as 'beliefs and ideas about what kinds of goals members of an organization should pursue and ideas about the appropriate kinds or standards of behavior organizational members should use to achieve these goals. From organizational values develop organizational norms, guidelines or expectations that prescribe appropriate kinds of behavior by employees in particular situations and control the behavior of organizational members towards one another.'

_____ is not the same as corporate culture.

   a. A Stake in the Outcome
   b. AAAI
   c. A4e
   d. Organizational culture

Chapter 8. Leadership Behavior

23. _____ is a method of directing, instructing and training a person or group of people, with the aim to achieve some goal or develop specific skills. There are many ways to coach, types of _____ and methods to _____. Direction may include motivational speaking.
    a. 1990 Clean Air Act
    b. Co-coaching
    c. 28-hour day
    d. Coaching

24. In psychology, _____ is a major approach to the study of human personality. Trait theorists are primarily interested in the measurement of traits, which can be defined as habitual patterns of behavior, thought, and emotion. According to this perspective, traits are relatively stable over time, differ among individuals (e.g. some people are outgoing whereas others are shy), and influence behavior.
    a. Groupthink
    b. Beck Depression Inventory
    c. Positive psychology
    d. Trait theory

25. _____ is the imitation of some real thing, state of affairs, or process. The act of simulating something generally entails representing certain key characteristics or behaviours of a selected physical or abstract system.

    _____ is used in many contexts, including the modeling of natural systems or human systems in order to gain insight into their functioning.

    a. Simulation
    b. 28-hour day
    c. 1990 Clean Air Act
    d. 33 Strategies of War

26. Social _____ is a social psychological and sociological perspective that explains social change and stability as a process of negotiated exchanges between parties. Social _____ posits that all human relationships are formed by the use of a subjective cost-benefit analysis and the comparison of alternatives. For example, when a person perceives the costs of a relationship as outweighing the perceived benefits, then the theory predicts that the person will choose to leave the relationship.
    a. A4e
    b. AAAI
    c. Exchange theory
    d. A Stake in the Outcome

Chapter 8. Leadership Behavior

27. Leadership is one of the primary areas of study, research, and practice in organizational behavior. Leaders often develop relationships with each member of the group that they lead, and _____ explains how those relationships with various members can develop in unique ways.

The _____ of leadership focuses on the two-way relationship between supervisors and subordinates.

   a. Groups decision making
   b. Human Centered Systems
   c. Light curtains
   d. Leader-Member Exchange theory

28. A _____ or chief executive is one of the highest-ranking corporate officer (executive) or administrator in charge of total management. An individual selected as President and _____ of a corporation, company, organization, or agency, reports to the board of directors. In internal communication and press releases, many companies capitalize the term and those of other high positions, even when they are not proper nouns.

   a. Questionnaire
   b. Learning
   c. Bandwagon effect
   d. Chief executive officer

29. _____ is a book authored by Marcus Buckingham and Curt Coffman who try to offer solutions to better employee satisfaction with the help of examples of how the best managers handle employees. The book gained popularity among managers since its release. The subtitle of the book is: What the World's Greatest Managers Do Differently.

   a. Peter Principle
   b. First, Break All the Rules
   c. Downsize This
   d. Lateral thinking

30. There are two types of _____ relationships: formal and informal. Informal relationships develop on their own between partners. Formal _____, on the other hand, refers to assigned relationships, often associated with organizational _____ programs designed to promote employee development or to assist at-risk children and youth.

   a. Force field analysis
   b. Management by exception
   c. Mentoring
   d. Management by objectives

Chapter 8. Leadership Behavior

31. _____ is acquiring new knowledge, behaviors, skills, values, preferences or understanding, and may involve synthesizing different types of information. The ability to learn is possessed by humans, animals and some machines. Progress over time tends to follow _____ curves.
    a. Learning
    b. Learning curve
    c. Learning cycle
    d. Meta learning

32. More recently organizations have come to understand that leadership can also be developed by strengthening the connection between and alignment of the efforts of individual leaders and the systems through which they influence organizational operations. This has led to a differentiation between leader development and _____. Leader development focuses on the development of the leader, such as the personal attributes desired in a leader, desired ways of behaving, ways of thinking or feeling.
    a. Path-goal theory
    b. Pseudoconsensus
    c. Leadership development
    d. Group process consultation

33. _____ is any process of estimating or inferring how local policies, actions, or changes influences the state of the neighboring universe. It is an approach to problem solving that views 'problems' as parts of an overall system, rather than reacting to present outcomes or events and potentially contributing to further development of the undesired issue or problem. _____ is a framework that is based on the belief that the component parts of a system can best be understood in the context of relationships with each other and with other systems, rather than in isolation.
    a. Sociotechnical systems theory
    b. Systems theory
    c. Subsystems
    d. Systems thinking

34. The _____ is a paradox in which a group of people collectively decide on a course of action that is counter to the preferences of any of the individuals in the group. It involves a common breakdown of group communication in which each member mistakenly believes that their own preferences are counter to the group's and, therefore, does not raise objections.
    a. A4e
    b. Abilene paradox
    c. A Stake in the Outcome
    d. AAAI

35. _____ is the term used to describe an act of a person in knowingly standing by without raising any objection to infringement of his rights, when someone else is unknowingly and honestly putting in his resources under the impression that the said rights actually belong to him. Consequently, the person whose rights are infringed cannot anymore make a claim against the infringer or succeed in an injunction suit due to his conduct. The term is most generally, 'permission' given by silence or passiveness.

 a. A4e
 b. A Stake in the Outcome
 c. Ownership
 d. Acquiescence

36. In psychology, as well as other social and behavioral sciences, _____ refers to behavior between members of the same species that is intended to cause pain or harm. Predatory or defensive behavior between members of different species is not normally considered '_____.' _____ takes a variety of forms among humans and can be physical, mental, or verbal. _____ should not be confused with assertiveness, although the terms are often used interchangeably among laypeople, e.g. an aggressive salesperson.

 a. A Stake in the Outcome
 b. A4e
 c. AAAI
 d. Aggression

37. _____ is a trait taught by many personal development experts and psychotherapists and the subject of many popular self-help books. It is linked to self-esteem and considered an important communication skill.

As a communication style and strategy, _____ is distinguished from aggression and passivity.

 a. Intrinsic motivation
 b. A4e
 c. A Stake in the Outcome
 d. Assertiveness

38. _____ is the amelioration of stress, especially chronic stress.

Walter Cannon and Hans Selye used animal studies to establish the earliest scientific basis for the study of stress. They measured the physiological responses of animals to external pressures, such as heat and cold, prolonged restraint, and surgical procedures, then extrapolated from these studies to human beings.

Chapter 8. Leadership Behavior

a. Stress management
b. 28-hour day
c. Labeling
d. 1990 Clean Air Act

39. _____ or self identity refers to the global understanding a sentient being has of him or herself. It presupposes but can be distinguished from self-consciousness, which is simply an awareness of one's self. It is also more general than self-esteem, which is the purely evaluative element of the _____.

a. Programmed instruction
b. Goal theory
c. Learning theories
d. Self-concept

40. A _____ is a brief written statement of the purpose of a company or organization. Ideally, a _____ guides the actions of the organization, spells out its overall goal, provides a sense of direction, and guides decision making for all levels of management.

_____s often contain the following:

- Purpose and aim of the organization
- The organization's primary stakeholders: clients, stockholders, etc.
- Responsibilities of the organization toward these stakeholders
- Products and services offered

In developing a _____:

- Encourage as much input as feasible from employees, volunteers, and other stakeholders
- Publicize it broadly
- Limit to a few statements.

The _____ can be used to resolve differences between business stakeholders.

a. 1990 Clean Air Act
b. 28-hour day
c. 33 Strategies of War
d. Mission statement

41. _____ is the set of reasons that determines one to engage in a particular behavior. The term is generally used for human _____ but, theoretically, it can be used to describe the causes for animal behavior as well

Chapter 8. Leadership Behavior **55**

a. Losada Zone
b. Work behavior
c. Motivation
d. Losada line

42. _____ involves establishing specific, measurable and time-targeted objectives. Work on the theory of goal-setting suggests that it's an effective tool for making progress by ensuring that participants in a group with a common goal are clearly aware of what is expected from them if an objective is to be achieved. On a personal level, setting goals is a process that allows people to specify then work towards their own objectives - most commonly with financial or career-based goals.

   a. Best practice
   b. Management Development
   c. Goal setting
   d. Theory X and theory Y

43. _____ is the practice of imposing something unpleasant or aversive on a person or animal, usually in response to disobedience, defiance governmental which is recorded in English since 1340, deriving from Old French puniss-, an extended form of the stem of punir 'to punish,' from Latin punire 'inflict a penalty on, cause pain for some offense,' earlier poenire, from poena 'penalty, _____ of great loss' .

Colloquial use of to punish for 'to inflict heavy damage or loss' is first recorded in 1801, originally in boxing; for punishing as 'hard-hitting' is from 1811.

   a. 33 Strategies of War
   b. Punishment
   c. 1990 Clean Air Act
   d. 28-hour day

44. _____ refers to the objective and subjective components of the believability of a source or message.

Traditionally, _____ has two key components: trustworthiness and expertise, which both have objective and subjective components. Trustworthiness is a based more on subjective factors, but can include objective measurements such as established reliability.

   a. 1990 Clean Air Act
   b. 28-hour day
   c. 33 Strategies of War
   d. Credibility

Chapter 8. Leadership Behavior

45. _____ are theories of human motivation created and developed by Douglas McGregor at the MIT Sloan School of Management in the 1960s that have been used in human resource management, organizational behavior, organizational communication and organizational development. They describe two very different attitudes toward workforce motivation. McGregor felt that companies followed either one or the other approach.

The first approach which many managers practice, management assumes employees are inherently lazy and will avoid work if they can. They inherently dislike work. Because of this, workers need to be closely supervised and comprehensive systems of controls developed.

In the second approach, management assumes employees may be ambitious and self-motivated and exercise self-control. It is believed that employees enjoy their mental and physical work duties.

   a. Resource-based view
   b. Management by exception
   c. Senior management
   d. Theory X and theory Y

46. In psychology, the 'Big Five' personality traits are five broad factors or dimensions of personality developed through lexical analysis. This is the rational and statistical analysis of words related to personality as found in natural-language dictionaries. The traits are also referred to as the '_____'.
   a. Conformity
   b. Groupthink
   c. Behaviorism
   d. Five Factor Model

Chapter 9. Motivation, Satisfaction, and Performance

1. The _____ provides a variety of management consulting, human resources and statistical research services. It has over 40 offices in 27 countries. World headquarters are in Washington, D.C.; operational headquarters are in Omaha, Nebraska.
   a. 1990 Clean Air Act
   b. 33 Strategies of War
   c. Gallup Organization
   d. 28-hour day

2. _____ is the set of reasons that determines one to engage in a particular behavior. The term is generally used for human _____ but, theoretically, it can be used to describe the causes for animal behavior as well
   a. Work behavior
   b. Motivation
   c. Losada Zone
   d. Losada line

3. An _____ is a social arrangement which pursues collective goals, which controls its own performance, and which has a boundary separating it from its environment. The word itself is derived from the Greek word ά½„ργανον (organon [itself derived from the better-known word ά¼"ργον ergon - work; deed - > ergonomics, etc]) meaning tool. The term is used in both daily and scientific English in multiple ways.
   a. Enron Corporation
   b. Investment
   c. American Psychological Society
   d. Organization

4. _____ describes how content an individual is with his or her job.
The happier people are within their job, the more satisfied they are said to be. _____ is not the same as motivation, although it is clearly linked.

   a. Graduate recruitment
   b. Resource dependence
   c. Life Orientations Training
   d. Job satisfaction

5. In economics, the term _____ refers to situations where the advancement of a qualified person within the hierarchy of an organization is stopped at a lower level because of some form of discrimination, most commonly sexism or racism, but since the term was coined, '_____' has also come to describe the limited advancement of the deaf, blind, disabled, aged and sexual minorities. It is an unofficial, invisible barrier that prevents women and minorities from advancing in businesses.

This situation is referred to as a 'ceiling' as there is a limitation blocking upward advancement, and 'glass' (transparent) because the limitation is not immediately apparent and is normally an unwritten and unofficial policy. This invisible barrier continues to exist, even though there are no explicit obstacles keeping minorities from acquiring advanced job positions - there are no advertisements that specifically say 'no minorities hired at this establishment', nor are there any formal orders that say 'minorities are not qualified' - but they do lie beneath the surface.

a. Glass ceiling
b. 1990 Clean Air Act
c. 33 Strategies of War
d. 28-hour day

6. _____ are a special type of work behavior that are defined as individual behaviors that are beneficial to the organization and are discretionary, not directly or explicitly recognized by the formal reward system. These behaviors are rather a matter of personal choice, such that their omission are not generally understood as punishable. _____s are thought to have an important impact on the effectiveness and efficiency of work teams and organizations, therefore contributing to the overall productivity of the organization.

a. A Stake in the Outcome
b. A4e
c. AAAI
d. Organizational citizenship behaviors

7. _____ in economics refers to metrics and measures of output from production processes, per unit of input. Labor _____, for example, is typically measured as a ratio of output per labor-hour, an input. _____ may be conceived of as a metrics of the technical or engineering efficiency of production.

a. Scientific management
b. 1990 Clean Air Act
c. 28-hour day
d. Productivity

8. _____ refers to increasing the spiritual, political, social or economic strength of individuals and communities. It often involves the empowered developing confidence in their own capacities.

The term Human _____ covers a vast landscape of meanings, interpretations, definitions and disciplines ranging from psychology and philosophy to the highly commercialized Self-Help industry and Motivational sciences.

a. Institutionalisation
b. Empowerment
c. Emotional labor
d. Institutionalization

9. Social _____ is a social psychological and sociological perspective that explains social change and stability as a process of negotiated exchanges between parties. Social _____ posits that all human relationships are formed by the use of a subjective cost-benefit analysis and the comparison of alternatives. For example, when a person perceives the costs of a relationship as outweighing the perceived benefits, then the theory predicts that the person will choose to leave the relationship.

a. AAAI
b. Exchange theory
c. A Stake in the Outcome
d. A4e

10. Leadership is one of the primary areas of study, research, and practice in organizational behavior. Leaders often develop relationships with each member of the group that they lead, and _____ explains how those relationships with various members can develop in unique ways.

The _____ of leadership focuses on the two-way relationship between supervisors and subordinates.

a. Leader-Member Exchange theory
b. Groups decision making
c. Human Centered Systems
d. Light curtains

11. More recently organizations have come to understand that leadership can also be developed by strengthening the connection between and alignment of the efforts of individual leaders and the systems through which they influence organizational operations. This has led to a differentiation between leader development and _____. Leader development focuses on the development of the leader, such as the personal attributes desired in a leader, desired ways of behaving, ways of thinking or feeling.

a. Path-goal theory
b. Group process consultation
c. Leadership development
d. Pseudoconsensus

Chapter 9. Motivation, Satisfaction, and Performance

12. Cognition is the scientific term for 'the process of thought'. Its usage varies in different ways in accord with different disciplines: For example, in psychology and _____ science it refers to an information processing view of an individual's psychological functions. Other interpretations of the meaning of cognition link it to the development of concepts; individual minds, groups, organizations, and even larger coalitions of entities, can be modelled as 'societies' (Society of Mind), which cooperate to form concepts.

   a. Disabilities
   b. Generation Y
   c. Cognitive processes
   d. Cognitive

13. Clayton Paul Alderfer is an American psychologist who further expanded Maslow's hierarchy of needs by categorizing the hierarchy into his _____ Alderfer categorized the lower order needs (Physiological and Safety) into the Existence category. He fit Maslow's interpersonal love and esteem needs into the relatedness category.

   Alderfer also proposed a regression theory to go along with the _____. He said that when needs in a higher category are not met then individuals redouble the efforts invested in a lower category need.

   a. ERG theory
   b. Affiliation
   c. Abraham Harold Maslow
   d. Adam Smith

14. _____ attempts to explain relational satisfaction in terms of perceptions of fair/unfair distributions of resources within interpersonal relationships. _____ is considered as one of the justice theories, It was first developed in 1962 by John Stacey Adams, a workplace and behavioral psychologist, who asserted that employees seek to maintain equity between the inputs that they bring to a job and the outcomes that they receive from it against the perceived inputs and outcomes of others (Adams, 1965.) The belief is that people value fair treatment which causes them to be motivated to keep the fairness maintained within the relationships of their co-workers and the organization.

   a. A4e
   b. A Stake in the Outcome
   c. AAAI
   d. Equity theory

15. _____ theory is about the mental processes regarding choice, or choosing. It explains the processes that an individual undergoes to make choices. In organizational behavior study, _____ theory is a motivation theory first proposed by Victor Vroom of the Yale School of Management.

a. Expectancy theory
b. Individual differences
c. A Stake in the Outcome
d. Expectancy

16. _____ is about the mental processes regarding choice, or choosing. It explains the processes that an individual undergoes to make choices. In organizational behavior study, _____ is a motivation theory first proposed by Victor Vroom of the Yale School of Management.
   a. Expectancy
   b. Individual differences
   c. A Stake in the Outcome
   d. Expectancy theory

17. A _____ or objective is a projected state of affairs that a person or a system plans or intends to achieve--a personal or organizational desired end-point in some sort of assumed development. Many people endeavor to reach _____ s within a finite time by setting deadlines.

A desire or an intention becomes a _____ if and only if one activates an action for achieving it

   a. Task list
   b. Management by exception
   c. Span of control
   d. Goal

18. _____ involves establishing specific, measurable and time-targeted objectives. Work on the theory of goal-setting suggests that it's an effective tool for making progress by ensuring that participants in a group with a common goal are clearly aware of what is expected from them if an objective is to be achieved. On a personal level, setting goals is a process that allows people to specify then work towards their own objectives - most commonly with financial or career-based goals.
   a. Best practice
   b. Goal setting
   c. Management Development
   d. Theory X and theory Y

19. Maslow's _____ is a theory in psychology, proposed by Abraham Maslow in his 1943 paper A Theory of Human Motivation, which he subsequently extended to include his observations of humans' innate curiosity.

Chapter 9. Motivation, Satisfaction, and Performance

Maslow studied what he called exemplary people such as Albert Einstein, Jane Addams, Eleanor Roosevelt, and Frederick Douglass rather than mentally ill or neurotic people, writing that 'the study of crippled, stunted, immature, and unhealthy specimens can yield only a cripple psychology and a cripple philosophy.' Maslow also studied the healthiest one percent of the college student population. In his book, The Farther Reaches of Human Nature, Maslow writes, 'By ordinary standards of this kind of laboratory research...

a. 1990 Clean Air Act
b. Hierarchy of needs
c. 33 Strategies of War
d. 28-hour day

20. _____ psychology focuses on this second level of study. It is also sometimes called Differential Psychology because researchers in this area study the ways in which individual people differ in their behavior. This is distinguished from other aspects of psychology in that although psychology is ostensibly a study of individuals, modern psychologists often study groups or biological underpinnings of cognition.
a. A Stake in the Outcome
b. Expectancy theory
c. Expectancy
d. Individual differences

21. The term _____ denotes a property of some thing or action which is essential and specific to that thing or action, and which is wholly independent of any other object, action or consequence. A characteristic which is not essential or inherent is extrinsic.

For example in biology, _____ effects originate from 'inside' an organism or cell, such as an autoimmune disease or _____ immunity.

a. A4e
b. AAAI
c. A Stake in the Outcome
d. Intrinsic

22. _____ comes from rewards inherent to a task or activity itself - the enjoyment of a puzzle or the love of playing basketball, for example. One is said to be intrinsically motivated when engaging in an activity 'with no apparent reward except for the activity itself'. This form of motivation has been studied by social and educational psychologists since the early 1970s.

a. A Stake in the Outcome
b. Extrinsic motivation
c. A4e
d. Intrinsic motivation

23. _____ was developed by Frederick Herzberg, a psychologist who found that job satisfaction and job dissatisfaction acted independently of each other. Two Factor Theory states that there are certain factors in the workplace that cause job satisfaction, while a separate set of factors cause dissatisfaction .

Attitudes and their connection with industrial mental health are related to Maslow's theory of motivation.

a. Need for achievement
b. Mortality salience
c. Holland Codes
d. Two-factor theory

24. _____ is a term used to described a tendency or preference towards a particular perspective, ideology or result, especially when the tendency interferes with the ability to be impartial, unprejudiced, or objective. The term _____ed is used to describe an action, judgment, or other outcome influenced by a prejudged perspective. It is also used to refer to a person or body of people whose actions or judgments exhibit _____.

a. 33 Strategies of War
b. 28-hour day
c. Bias
d. 1990 Clean Air Act

25. The _____ occurs when an external incentive such as money or prizes decreases a person's intrinsic motivation to perform a task. According to self-perception theory, people pay more attention to the incentive, and less attention to the enjoyment and satisfaction that they receive from performing the activity. The overall effect is a shift in motivation to extrinsic factors and the undermining of pre-existing intrinsic motivation.

a. Overjustification effect
b. A4e
c. AAAI
d. A Stake in the Outcome

26. _____ Stores, Inc. is an American public corporation that runs a chain of large, discount department stores. It is the world's largest public corporation by revenue, according to the 2008 Fortune Global 500.

a. Adam Smith
b. William Edwards Deming
c. Wal-Mart
d. Abraham Harold Maslow

27. The _____ refers to situations in which students perform better than other students simply because they are expected to do so. The effect is named after George Bernard Shaw's play Pygmalion, in which a professor makes a bet that he can teach a poor flower girl to speak and act like an upper-class lady, and is successful.

The _____ requires a student to internalize the expectations of their superiors.

a. Group-serving bias
b. Halo effect
c. Confirmation bias
d. Pygmalion Effect

28. The _____ is a performance management tool for measuring whether the smaller-scale operational activities of a company are aligned with its larger-scale objectives in terms of vision and strategy.

By focusing not only on financial outcomes but also on the operational, marketing and developmental inputs to these, the _____ helps provide a more comprehensive view of a business, which in turn helps organizations act in their best long-term interests. This tool is also being used to address business response to climate change and greenhouse gas emissions.

a. Balanced Scorecard
b. Time management
c. Management Development
d. Performance improvement

29. _____ is the belief that one is capable of performing in a certain manner to attain certain goals. It is a belief that one has the capabilities to execute the courses of actions required to manage prospective situations. Unlike efficacy, which is the power to produce an effect (in essence, competence), _____ is the belief (whether or not accurate) that one has the power to produce that effect.

a. Positive psychological capital
b. 1990 Clean Air Act
c. Self-efficacy
d. 28-hour day

Chapter 9. Motivation, Satisfaction, and Performance

30. _____ is a method of directing, instructing and training a person or group of people, with the aim to achieve some goal or develop specific skills. There are many ways to coach, types of _____ and methods to _____. Direction may include motivational speaking.
    a. Coaching
    b. Co-coaching
    c. 28-hour day
    d. 1990 Clean Air Act

31. In economics, _____ is the desire to own something and the ability to pay for it. The term _____ signifies the ability or the willingness to buy a particular commodity at a given point of time.
    a. Demand
    b. 33 Strategies of War
    c. 28-hour day
    d. 1990 Clean Air Act

32. A _____ is a form of periodic payment from an employer to an employee, which may be specified in an employment contract. It is contrasted with piece wages, where each job, hour or other unit is paid separately, rather than on a periodic basis.

    From the point of a view of running a business, _____ can also be viewed as the cost of acquiring human resources for running operations, and is then termed personnel expense or _____ expense.

    a. War for talent
    b. Trust fall
    c. Salary
    d. Continuing professional development

33. _____ is the practice of imposing something unpleasant or aversive on a person or animal, usually in response to disobedience, defiance governmental which is recorded in English since 1340, deriving from Old French puniss-, an extended form of the stem of punir 'to punish,' from Latin punire 'inflict a penalty on, cause pain for some offense,' earlier poenire, from poena 'penalty, _____ of great loss' .

Colloquial use of to punish for 'to inflict heavy damage or loss' is first recorded in 1801, originally in boxing; for punishing as 'hard-hitting' is from 1811.

a. 28-hour day
b. 33 Strategies of War
c. 1990 Clean Air Act
d. Punishment

34. In psychology, _____ reflects a person's overall evaluation or appraisal of his or her own worth.

_____ encompasses beliefs (for example, 'I am competent/incompetent') and emotions (for example, triumph/despair, pride/shame.) Behavior may reflect _____

a. 1990 Clean Air Act
b. Self-esteem
c. 33 Strategies of War
d. 28-hour day

35. The sociologist Max Weber defined _____ as 'resting on devotion to the exceptional sanctity, heroism or exemplary character of an individual person, and of the normative patterns or order revealed or ordained by him.' _____ is one of three forms of authority laid out in Weber's tripartite classification of authority, the other two being traditional authority and rational-legal authority. The concept has acquired wide usage among sociologists.

In his writings about _____, Weber applies the term charisma to 'a certain quality of an individual personality, by virtue of which he is set apart from ordinary men and treated as endowed with supernatural, superhuman, or at least specifically exceptional powers or qualities.

a. 1990 Clean Air Act
b. 33 Strategies of War
c. 28-hour day
d. Charismatic authority

36. _____ is a leadership style that defines as leadership that creates voluble and positive change in the followers. A transformational leader focuses on 'transforming' others to help each other, to look out for each other, be encouraging, harmonious, and look out for the organization as a whole. In this leadership, the leader enhances the motivation, moral and performance of his follower group.
a. Need for affiliation
b. Milgram experiment
c. Subpersonality
d. Transformational leadership

37. In a human resources context, _____ or labor _____ is the rate at which an employer gains and loses employees. Simple ways to describe it are 'how long employees tend to stay' or 'the rate of traffic through the revolving door.' _____ is measured for individual companies and for their industry as a whole. If an employer is said to have a high _____ relative to its competitors, it means that employees of that company have a shorter average tenure than those of other companies in the same industry.
   a. Crisis management
   b. Professional communication
   c. Turnover
   d. Rosenberg self-esteem scale

38. A _____ is a sociological concept referring to a group to which an individual or another group is compared.

   _____s are used in order to evaluate and determine the nature of a given individual or other group's characteristics and sociological attributes. It is the group to which the individual relates or aspires relate himself or self psychologically.

   a. Social network
   b. Dehumanization
   c. Reference group
   d. Moral panic

39. Negative Affect is a general dimension of subjective distress and unpleasurable engagement that subsumes a variety of aversive mood states, including anger, contempt, disgust, guilt, fear, and nervousness. Individuals high in _____ are characterized by distress, un-pleasurable engagement, and nervousness. Low negative affect is characterised by a state of calmness and serenity.
   a. Source credibility
   b. Care perspective
   c. Differential item functioning
   d. Negative affectivity

40. Positive Affect reflects the extent to which a person feels enthusiastic, active, and alert. High _____ is a state of high energy, full concentration, and pleasurable engagement, whereas low _____ is characterized by sadness, lethargy, distress, and un-pleasurable engagement.

Watson and Clark defined _____ as reflecting pervasive individual differences in positive emotionality and self-concept.

a. Four Temperaments
b. Psychology of Selves
c. Personality pathology
d. Positive affectivity

41. _____ are job factors that can cause dissatisfaction if missing but do not necessarily motivate employees if increased.

_____ have mostly to do with the job environment. These factors are important or notable only when they are lacking.

a. Cover letter
b. Hygiene factors
c. Work system
d. Performance improvement plan

42. _____ concerns what is just or right with respect to the allocation of goods in a society. Thus, a community whose individual members are rendered their due would be considered a society guided by the principles of _____. Allocation of goods takes into thought the total amount of goods to be handed out, the process on how they in the civilization are going to dispense, and the pattern of division.

a. 28-hour day
b. Distributive justice
c. 1990 Clean Air Act
d. 33 Strategies of War

43. _____ is defined by sociologist John R. Schermerhorn as the '...degree to which the people affected by decision are treated by dignity and respect. (John R. Schermerhorn, Organizational behavior) The theory focuses on the interpersonal treatment people receive when procedures are implemented.

_____ has come to be seen as consisting of two specific types of interpersonal treatment (e.g. Greenberg, 1990a, 1993b).

a. Employeeship
b. On-Ramping
c. Illness rate
d. Interactional justice

44. _____ is the study of people's perception of fairness in organizations.

Chapter 9. Motivation, Satisfaction, and Performance

Organizational literature tends to focus on three specific forms of justice perceptions:

- Distributive justice considers perceptions of fairness of outcomes (equity, equality, and needs)
- Procedural justice emphasises the importance of fairness of the methods or procedures used (decision criteria, voice, control of the process)
- Interactional justice is based on the perceived fairness of the interpersonal treatment received, whether those involved are treated wish sensitivity, dignity and respect, and also the nature of the explanations given.

These vary depending on the method or nature of justice being assessed or practiced in the organization.

Generally, maintaining good _____ can lead to ideal and favourable outcomes in the workplace. It is expected that employees will act according to organizational rules and regulations if they are treating fairly and receive the outcomes they desire.

   a. A Stake in the Outcome
   b. Organizational justice
   c. AAAI
   d. A4e

45. _____ refers to the idea of fairness in the processes that resolve disputes and allocate resources. One aspect of _____ is related to discussions of the administration of justice and legal proceedings. This sense of _____ is connected to due process (U.S.), fundamental justice (Canada), procedural fairness (Australia) and natural justice (other Common law jurisdictions), but the idea of _____ can also be applied to nonlegal contexts in which some process is employed to resolve conflict or divide benefits or burdens.
   a. 1990 Clean Air Act
   b. 33 Strategies of War
   c. 28-hour day
   d. Procedural justice

Chapter 10. Groups, Teams and Their Leadership

1. _____ is a dynamic of being mutually and physically responsible to and sharing a common set of principles with others. This concept differs distinctly from 'dependence' in that an interdependent relationship implies that all participants are emotionally, economically, ecologically and or morally 'interdependent.' Some people advocate freedom or independence as a sort of ultimate good; others do the same with devotion to one's family, community, or society. _____ recognizes the truth in each position and weaves them together.

    a. AAAI
    b. Interdependence
    c. A Stake in the Outcome
    d. A4e

2. An _____ is a social arrangement which pursues collective goals, which controls its own performance, and which has a boundary separating it from its environment. The word itself is derived from the Greek word ἄργανον (organon [itself derived from the better-known word ἔργον ergon - work; deed - > ergonomics, etc]) meaning tool. The term is used in both daily and scientific English in multiple ways.

    a. American Psychological Society
    b. Enron Corporation
    c. Investment
    d. Organization

3. _____ is a term originating in military organization theory, but now used more commonly in business management, particularly human resource management. _____ refers to the number of subordinates a supervisor has.

    In the hierarchical business organization of the past it was not uncommon to see average spans of 1 to 10 or even less.

    a. Job enrichment
    b. Professional development
    c. Mentoring
    d. Span of control

4. _____ is a concept in ethics with several meanings. It is often used synonymously with such concepts as responsibility, answerability, enforcement, blameworthiness, liability and other terms associated with the expectation of account-giving. As an aspect of governance, it has been central to discussions related to problems in both the public and private (corporation) worlds.

    a. A4e
    b. AAAI
    c. A Stake in the Outcome
    d. Accountability

Chapter 10. Groups, Teams and Their Leadership

5. _____ is the tendency for people to be aroused into better performance on simple tasks (or tasks at which they are expert or that have become autonomous) when under the eye of others, rather than while they are alone (audience effect) however, are often performed in an inferior manner in such situations. This effect has been demonstrated in a variety of species.

   a. Contact hypothesis
   b. Dump job
   c. Social facilitation
   d. Machiavellianism

6. In the social psychology of groups, _____ is the phenomenon of people making less effort to achieve a goal when they work in a group than when they work alone. This is seen as one of the main reasons groups are sometimes less productive than the combined performance of their members working as individuals.

   - Ringelmann, Max : 1913

   Research began in 1913 with Max Ringelmann's study. He found that when he asked a group of men to pull on a rope, that they did not pull as hard, or put as much effort into the activity, as they did when they were pulling alone.

   a. Hysterical contagion
   b. Role theory
   c. Contact hypothesis
   d. Social loafing

7. The _____ is a form of reactivity whereby subjects improve an aspect of their behavior being experimentally measured simply in response to the fact that they are being studied, not in response to any particular experimental manipulation.

   The term was coined in 1955 by Henry A. Landsberger when analyzing older experiments from 1924-1932 at the Hawthorne Works (outside Chicago.) Hawthorne Works had commissioned a study to see if its workers would become more productive in higher or lower levels of light.

   a. 28-hour day
   b. 33 Strategies of War
   c. 1990 Clean Air Act
   d. Hawthorne effect

8. A _____ is a team whose members usually belong to different groups, functions and are assigned to activities for the same project. A team can be divided into sub-teams according to need. Usually _____s are only used for a defined period of time.

Chapter 10. Groups, Teams and Their Leadership

a. 1990 Clean Air Act
b. 33 Strategies of War
c. 28-hour day
d. Project team

9. _____ is a theory in evolutionary biology which states that most sexually reproducing species experience little change for most of their geological history, showing stasis in the fossil record, and that when phenotypic evolution does occur, it is localized in rare, rapid events of branching speciation (called cladogenesis.)

_____ is commonly contrasted against the theory of phyletic gradualism, which states that evolution generally occurs uniformly and by the steady and gradual transformation of whole lineages (anagenesis.) In this view, evolution is seen as generally smooth and continuous.

a. Coevolution
b. Homologous
c. Punctuated equilibrium
d. Hopeful monster

10. _____ is a method of directing, instructing and training a person or group of people, with the aim to achieve some goal or develop specific skills. There are many ways to coach, types of _____ and methods to _____. Direction may include motivational speaking.
a. Co-coaching
b. 1990 Clean Air Act
c. Coaching
d. 28-hour day

11. The _____ was a study of the psychological effects of becoming a prisoner or prison guard. The experiment was conducted in 1971 by a team of researchers led by Psychology Professor Philip Zimbardo at Stanford University. Twenty-four undergraduates were selected out of 70 to play the roles of both guards and prisoners and live in a mock prison in the basement of the Stanford psychology building. Those selected were chosen for their lack of psychological issues, crime history, and medical disabilities, in order to obtain a representative sample. Roles were assigned based on a coin toss.

Prisoners and guards rapidly adapted to their roles, stepping beyond the boundaries of what had been predicted and leading to dangerous and psychologically damaging situations. One-third of the guards were judged to have exhibited 'genuine' sadistic tendencies, while many prisoners were emotionally traumatized and two had to be removed from the experiment early.

Chapter 10. Groups, Teams and Their Leadership   73

   a. 33 Strategies of War
   b. 28-hour day
   c. 1990 Clean Air Act
   d. Stanford Prison experiment

12. _____ refers to the long-term management of intractable conflicts. It is the label for the variety of ways by which people handle grievances--standing up for what they consider to be right and against what they consider to be wrong. Those ways include such diverse phenomena as gossip, ridicule, lynching, terrorism, warfare, feuding, genocide, law, mediation, and avoidance.
   a. 33 Strategies of War
   b. 1990 Clean Air Act
   c. Conflict management
   d. 28-hour day

13. '_____ is a conflict among the roles corresponding to two or more statuses.'

   _____ is a special form of social conflict that takes place when one is forced to take on two different and incompatible roles at the same time. Consider the example of a doctor who is himself a patient, or who must decide whether he should be present for his daughter's birthday party (in his role as 'father') or attend an ailing patient (as 'doctor'.) (Also compare the psychological concept of cognitive dissonance.)

   a. Spheres of influence
   b. Social constructionism
   c. Reference group
   d. Role conflict

14. _____ is a type of thought exhibited by group members who try to minimize conflict and reach consensus without critically testing, analyzing, and evaluating ideas. Individual creativity, uniqueness, and independent thinking are lost in the pursuit of group cohesiveness, as are the advantages of reasonable balance in choice and thought that might normally be obtained by making decisions as a group. During _____, members of the group avoid promoting viewpoints outside the comfort zone of consensus thinking.
   a. Groupthink
   b. Diffusion of responsibility
   c. Social cognitive theory
   d. Self-report inventory

Chapter 10. Groups, Teams and Their Leadership

15. The sociologist Max Weber defined _____ as 'resting on devotion to the exceptional sanctity, heroism or exemplary character of an individual person, and of the normative patterns or order revealed or ordained by him.' _____ is one of three forms of authority laid out in Weber's tripartite classification of authority, the other two being traditional authority and rational-legal authority. The concept has acquired wide usage among sociologists.

In his writings about _____, Weber applies the term charisma to 'a certain quality of an individual personality, by virtue of which he is set apart from ordinary men and treated as endowed with supernatural, superhuman, or at least specifically exceptional powers or qualities.

a. 33 Strategies of War
b. 28-hour day
c. 1990 Clean Air Act
d. Charismatic authority

16. _____ is the imitation of some real thing, state of affairs, or process. The act of simulating something generally entails representing certain key characteristics or behaviours of a selected physical or abstract system.

_____ is used in many contexts, including the modeling of natural systems or human systems in order to gain insight into their functioning.

a. 28-hour day
b. 33 Strategies of War
c. 1990 Clean Air Act
d. Simulation

17. _____ is a joint action by two or more people or a group, in which each person contributes with different skills and Express his or her individual interests and opinions to the unity and efficiency of the group in order to achieve common goals.

This does not mean that the individual is no longer important; however, it does mean that effective and efficient _____ goes beyond individual accomplishments. The most effective _____ is produced when all the individuals involved harmonize their contributions and work towards a common goal.

a. 28-hour day
b. 33 Strategies of War
c. 1990 Clean Air Act
d. Teamwork

18. A _____ is a brief written statement of the purpose of a company or organization. Ideally, a _____ guides the actions of the organization, spells out its overall goal, provides a sense of direction, and guides decision making for all levels of management.

Chapter 10. Groups, Teams and Their Leadership

_____s often contain the following:

- Purpose and aim of the organization
- The organization's primary stakeholders: clients, stockholders, etc.
- Responsibilities of the organization toward these stakeholders
- Products and services offered

In developing a _____:

- Encourage as much input as feasible from employees, volunteers, and other stakeholders
- Publicize it broadly
- Limit to a few statements.

The _____ can be used to resolve differences between business stakeholders.

a. 28-hour day
b. 1990 Clean Air Act
c. Mission statement
d. 33 Strategies of War

19. _____ is the state achieved by coming together, the state of agreement. The Latin congruere means to come together, agree. As an abstract term, _____ means similarity between objects.
a. Turnover
b. The Goodyear Tire ' Rubber Company
c. HMIS
d. Congruence

20. _____ is a term used to classify a group leadership theories that inquire the interactions between leaders and followers. A transactional leader focuses more on a series of 'transactions'. This person is interested in looking out for oneself, having exchange benefits with their subordinates and clarify a sense of duty with rewards and punishments to reach goals.
a. Reflective listening
b. Care perspective
c. Negative affectivity
d. Transactional leadership

Chapter 10. Groups, Teams and Their Leadership

21. _____ is a leadership style that defines as leadership that creates voluble and positive change in the followers. A transformational leader focuses on 'transforming' others to help each other, to look out for each other, be encouraging, harmonious, and look out for the organization as a whole. In this leadership, the leader enhances the motivation, moral and performance of his follower group.
    a. Subpersonality
    b. Milgram experiment
    c. Need for affiliation
    d. Transformational leadership

22. A _____ is a list of the general tasks and responsibilities of a position. Typically, it also includes to whom the position reports, specifications such as the qualifications needed by the person in the job, salary range for the position, etc. A _____ is usually developed by conducting a job analysis, which includes examining the tasks and sequences of tasks necessary to perform the job.
    a. Job description
    b. Labour hire
    c. Recruitment
    d. Referral recruitment

23. More recently organizations have come to understand that leadership can also be developed by strengthening the connection between and alignment of the efforts of individual leaders and the systems through which they influence organizational operations. This has led to a differentiation between leader development and _____. Leader development focuses on the development of the leader, such as the personal attributes desired in a leader, desired ways of behaving, ways of thinking or feeling.
    a. Group process consultation
    b. Pseudoconsensus
    c. Path-goal theory
    d. Leadership Development

24. The twelve _____ to intervene in a system were proposed by Donella Meadows, a scientist and system analyst focused on environmental limits to economic growth. The _____, first published in 1997, were inspired by her attendance at a North American Free Trade Agreement (NAFTA) meeting in the early 1990s where she realized that a very large new system was being proposed but the mechanisms to manage it were ineffective.

Meadows, who worked in the field of systems analysis, proposed a scale of places to intervene in a system.

Chapter 10. Groups, Teams and Their Leadership

a. 33 Strategies of War
b. Leverage points
c. 1990 Clean Air Act
d. 28-hour day

25. A _____ is the learned capacity to carry out pre-determined results often with the minimum outlay of time, energy, or both. _____s can often be divided into domain-general and domain-specific _____s. For example, in the domain of work, some general _____s would include time management, teamwork and leadership, self motivation and others, whereas domain-specific _____s would be useful only for a certain job.

a. 1990 Clean Air Act
b. 33 Strategies of War
c. Skill
d. 28-hour day

26. _____ is a typological term most closely associated with sociologist Max Weber. An _____ is formed from characteristics and elements of the given phenomena, but it is not meant to correspond to all of the characteristics of any one particular case. It is not meant to refer to perfect things, moral ideals nor to statistical averages but rather to stress certain elements common to most cases of the given phenomena.

a. A4e
b. AAAI
c. A Stake in the Outcome
d. Ideal type

27. _____ describes the situation when output from (or information about the result of) an event or phenomenon in the past will influence the same event/phenomenon in the present or future. When an event is part of a chain of cause-and-effect that forms a circuit or loop, then the event is said to 'feed back' into itself.

_____ is also a synonym for:

- _____ Signal; the information about the initial event that is the basis for subsequent modification of the event.
- _____ Loop; the causal path that leads from the initial generation of the _____ signal to the subsequent modification of the event.

_____ is a mechanism, process or signal that is looped back to control a system within itself. Such a loop is called a _____ loop.

Chapter 10. Groups, Teams and Their Leadership

a. 1990 Clean Air Act
b. 28-hour day
c. Feedback
d. Positive feedback

28. In economics, the term _____ refers to situations where the advancement of a qualified person within the hierarchy of an organization is stopped at a lower level because of some form of discrimination, most commonly sexism or racism, but since the term was coined, '_____' has also come to describe the limited advancement of the deaf, blind, disabled, aged and sexual minorities. It is an unofficial, invisible barrier that prevents women and minorities from advancing in businesses.

This situation is referred to as a 'ceiling' as there is a limitation blocking upward advancement, and 'glass' (transparent) because the limitation is not immediately apparent and is normally an unwritten and unofficial policy. This invisible barrier continues to exist, even though there are no explicit obstacles keeping minorities from acquiring advanced job positions - there are no advertisements that specifically say 'no minorities hired at this establishment', nor are there any formal orders that say 'minorities are not qualified' - but they do lie beneath the surface.

a. 33 Strategies of War
b. 1990 Clean Air Act
c. 28-hour day
d. Glass ceiling

29. A _____ -- also known as a geographically dispersed team -- is a group of individuals who work across time, space, and organizational boundaries with links strengthened by webs of communication technology. They have complementary skills and are committed to a common purpose, have interdependent performance goals, and share an approach to work for which they hold themselves mutually accountable. Geographically dispersed teams allow organizations to hire and retain the best people regardless of location.
a. 1990 Clean Air Act
b. Risk management
c. Succession planning
d. Virtual team

30. Social _____ is a social psychological and sociological perspective that explains social change and stability as a process of negotiated exchanges between parties. Social _____ posits that all human relationships are formed by the use of a subjective cost-benefit analysis and the comparison of alternatives. For example, when a person perceives the costs of a relationship as outweighing the perceived benefits, then the theory predicts that the person will choose to leave the relationship.

a. AAAI
b. A Stake in the Outcome
c. A4e
d. Exchange theory

31. Leadership is one of the primary areas of study, research, and practice in organizational behavior. Leaders often develop relationships with each member of the group that they lead, and _____ explains how those relationships with various members can develop in unique ways.

The _____ of leadership focuses on the two-way relationship between supervisors and subordinates.

   a. Leader-Member Exchange theory
   b. Groups decision making
   c. Human Centered Systems
   d. Light curtains

32. In contrast, positive feedback is a feedback in which the system responds in the same direction as the perturbation, resulting in amplification of the original signal instead of stabilizing the signal. A positive feedback of 100% or greater will result in a runaway situation. Both positive and _____ require a feedback loop to operate, as opposed to feedforward, which does not rely on a feedback loop for its control of the system.
   a. Positive feedback
   b. Negative feedback
   c. 1990 Clean Air Act
   d. 28-hour day

33. _____, sometimes referred to as 'cumulative causation', is a feedback loop system in which the system responds to perturbation in the same direction as the perturbation. In contrast, a system that responds to the perturbation in the opposite direction is called a negative feedback system. These concepts were first recognized as broadly applicable by Norbert Wiener in his 1948 work on cybernetics.
   a. Negative feedback
   b. 1990 Clean Air Act
   c. 28-hour day
   d. Positive feedback

Chapter 10. Groups, Teams and Their Leadership

34. _____ is the practice of imposing something unpleasant or aversive on a person or animal, usually in response to disobedience, defiance governmental which is recorded in English since 1340, deriving from Old French puniss-, an extended form of the stem of punir 'to punish,' from Latin punire 'inflict a penalty on, cause pain for some offense,' earlier poenire, from poena 'penalty, _____ of great loss' .

Colloquial use of to punish for 'to inflict heavy damage or loss' is first recorded in 1801, originally in boxing; for punishing as 'hard-hitting' is from 1811.

a. 1990 Clean Air Act
b. 33 Strategies of War
c. 28-hour day
d. Punishment

35. In the arts and antiques, _____ is the judgment by experts as to the authorship, date, or other aspect of the origin of a work of art or cultural artifact. Works 'attributed' to an artist are more firmly believed to be theirs than those 'ascribed'.

_____ can also mean:

- _____, a concept in copyright law requiring an author to be credited
- Journalism sourcing (or _____), a journalistic practice of attributing information to its source
- _____ (psychology), a concept in psychology whereby people attribute traits and causes to things they observe
- Performance _____, a technique in quantitative finance for explaining the active performance of a portfolio

a. A4e
b. Attribution
c. Ambition
d. A Stake in the Outcome

36. _____ is based on the proposition that all things which organisms do--including thinking and feeling--can and should be regarded as behaviors. The school of psychology maintains that behaviors as such can be described scientifically without recourse either to internal physiological events or to hypothetical constructs such as the mind. _____ comprises the position that all theories should have observational correlates but that there are no philosophical differences between publicly observable processes and privately observable processes

a. Conformity
b. Diffusion of responsibility
c. Psychometrics
d. Behaviorism

Chapter 10. Groups, Teams and Their Leadership   81

37. _____ describes how content an individual is with his or her job.

The happier people are within their job, the more satisfied they are said to be. _____ is not the same as motivation, although it is clearly linked.

   a. Life Orientations Training
   b. Graduate recruitment
   c. Job satisfaction
   d. Resource dependence

38. _____ is a habitual pattern of absence from a duty or obligation.

Frequent absence from the workplace may be indicative of poor morale or of sick building syndrome. However, many employers have implemented absence policies which make no distinction between absences for genuine illness and absence for inappropriate reasons.

   a. A4e
   b. Ownership
   c. Absenteeism
   d. A Stake in the Outcome

39. _____ is the practice of compelling a person or manipulating them to behave in an involuntary way by use of threats, intimidation, trickery, or some other form of pressure or force. These are used as leverage, to force the victim to act in the desired way. _____ may involve the actual infliction of physical pain/injury or psychological harm in order to enhance the credibility of a threat.

   a. 28-hour day
   b. Good faith
   c. Coercion
   d. 1990 Clean Air Act

40. _____ is individual power based on a high level of identification with, admiration of, or respect for the powerholder.

Nationalism, Patriotism, Celebrities and well-respected people are examples of _____ in effect.

_____ is one of the Five Bases of Social Power, as defined by Bertram Raven and his colleagues[1] in 1959.

a. Reflective listening
b. Convergent thinking
c. Transfer of training
d. Referent power

41. _____ is a social psychology theory developed by Fritz Heider, Harold Kelley, Edward E. Jones, and Lee Ross.

The theory is concerned with the ways in which people explain (or attribute) the behavior of others or themselves (self-attribution) with something else. It explores how individuals 'attribute' causes to events and how this cognitive perception effects their usefulness in an organization.

a. Attribution theory
b. AAAI
c. A Stake in the Outcome
d. A4e

42. _____ is a range of processes aimed at alleviating or eliminating sources of conflict. The term '_____' is sometimes used interchangeably with the term dispute resolution or alternative dispute resolution. Processes of _____ generally include negotiation, mediation and diplomacy.

a. 1990 Clean Air Act
b. 33 Strategies of War
c. Conflict resolution
d. 28-hour day

43. _____ is a concept found in moral, political, and bioethical philosophy. Within these contexts, it refers to the capacity of a rational individual to make an informed, un-coerced decision. In moral and political philosophy, _____ is often used as the basis for determining moral responsibility for one's actions.

a. AAAI
b. A4e
c. A Stake in the Outcome
d. Autonomy

44. A _____ is a research instrument consisting of a series of questions and other prompts for the purpose of gathering information from respondents. Although they are often designed for statistical analysis of the responses, this is not always the case. The _____ was invented by Sir Francis Galton.

Chapter 10. Groups, Teams and Their Leadership

a. Questionnaire
b. 28-hour day
c. 1990 Clean Air Act
d. Structured interview

45. _____ refers to the process of developing and integrating new workers, developing and retaining current workers, and attracting highly skilled workers to work for your company. _____ in this context does not refer to the management of entertainers

   a. Separation of duties
   b. Personnel management
   c. Human resource consulting
   d. Talent management

46. _____ is an intangible term used for the capacity of people to maintain belief in an institution or a goal, or even in oneself and others. The second term applies particularly to military personnel and to members of sports teams, but is also applicable in business and in any other organizational context, particularly in times of stress or controversy.

According to Alexander H. Leighton, '_____ is the capacity of a group of people to pull together persistently and consistently in pursuit of a common purpose'.

   a. 33 Strategies of War
   b. 1990 Clean Air Act
   c. 28-hour day
   d. Morale

47. A _____ or objective is a projected state of affairs that a person or a system plans or intends to achieve--a personal or organizational desired end-point in some sort of assumed development. Many people endeavor to reach _____s within a finite time by setting deadlines.

A desire or an intention becomes a _____ if and only if one activates an action for achieving it

   a. Goal
   b. Management by exception
   c. Task list
   d. Span of control

Chapter 10. Groups, Teams and Their Leadership

48. _____ involves establishing specific, measurable and time-targeted objectives. Work on the theory of goal-setting suggests that it's an effective tool for making progress by ensuring that participants in a group with a common goal are clearly aware of what is expected from them if an objective is to be achieved. On a personal level, setting goals is a process that allows people to specify then work towards their own objectives - most commonly with financial or career-based goals.

   a. Best practice
   b. Theory X and theory Y
   c. Goal setting
   d. Management Development

49. _____ asserts that there is a technique, method, process, activity, incentive or reward that is more effective at delivering a particular outcome than any other technique, method, process, etc. The idea is that with proper processes, checks, and testing, a desired outcome can be delivered with fewer problems and unforeseen complications. _____s can also be defined as the most efficient (least amount of effort) and effective (best results) way of accomplishing a task, based on repeatable procedures that have proven themselves over time for large numbers of people.

   a. Management by exception
   b. Best practice
   c. Span of control
   d. Contingency Theory

50. _____ is acquiring new knowledge, behaviors, skills, values, preferences or understanding, and may involve synthesizing different types of information. The ability to learn is possessed by humans, animals and some machines. Progress over time tends to follow _____ curves.

   a. Learning
   b. Meta learning
   c. Learning curve
   d. Learning cycle

51. _____ refers to the objective and subjective components of the believability of a source or message.

Traditionally, _____ has two key components: trustworthiness and expertise, which both have objective and subjective components. Trustworthiness is a based more on subjective factors, but can include objective measurements such as established reliability.

   a. 28-hour day
   b. 1990 Clean Air Act
   c. 33 Strategies of War
   d. Credibility

52. _____ refers to increasing the spiritual, political, social or economic strength of individuals and communities. It often involves the empowered developing confidence in their own capacities.

The term Human _____ covers a vast landscape of meanings, interpretations, definitions and disciplines ranging from psychology and philosophy to the highly commercialized Self-Help industry and Motivational sciences.

   a. Institutionalisation
   b. Emotional labor
   c. Empowerment
   d. Institutionalization

53. _____ can be regarded as an outcome of mental processes (cognitive process) leading to the selection of a course of action among several alternatives. Every _____ process produces a final choice. The output can be an action or an opinion of choice.
   a. Decision making
   b. 28-hour day
   c. 1990 Clean Air Act
   d. 33 Strategies of War

Chapter 11. Characteristics of the Situation

1. _____ is the state achieved by coming together, the state of agreement. The Latin congruere means to come together, agree. As an abstract term, _____ means similarity between objects.
   a. Congruence
   b. Turnover
   c. The Goodyear Tire ' Rubber Company
   d. HMIS

2. _____ is a class of behavioural theory that claims that there is no best way to organize a corporation, to lead a company, or to make decisions. Instead, the optimal course of action is contingent (dependant) upon the internal and external situation. Several contingency approaches were developed concurrently in the late 1960s.
   a. Resource-based view
   b. Senior management
   c. Goal setting
   d. Contingency Theory

3. _____ is a perspective in social psychology that considers most of everyday activity to be the acting out of socially defined categories (e.g., mother, manager, teacher.) Each social role is a universe of rights, duties, expectations, norms and behaviour a person has to face and to fulfill.

The theory posits the following propositions about social behaviour:

1. People spend much of their lives in groups.
2. Within these groups, people often take distinct positions.
3. Each of these positions can be called a role, with a whole set of functions that are molded by the expectations of others.
4. Formalized expectations become norms when enough people feel comfortable in providing punishments and rewards for the expected behavior.
5. People generally conform to their roles.
6. The anticipation of rewards and punishments inspire this conformity.

A key insight of this theory is that role conflict occurs when a person is expected to simultaneously act out multiple roles that carry contradictory expectations.

In sociology there are different categories of social roles:

1. cultural roles: roles given by culture (e.g. priest)
2. social differentiation: e.g. teacher, taxi driver
3. situation-specific roles: e.g. eye witness
4. bio-sociological roles: e.g. as human in a natural system
5. gender roles: as a man, woman, mother, father, etc.

Chapter 11. Characteristics of the Situation

In their life people have to face different social roles, sometimes they have to face different roles at the same time in different social situations. There is an evolution of social roles: some disappear and some new develop.

a. Role theory
b. Contact hypothesis
c. Locus of control
d. Social loafing

4. Organizational culture is not the same as _____. It is wider and deeper concepts, something that an organization 'is' rather than what it 'has' (according to Buchanan and Huczynski.)

_____ is the total sum of the values, customs, traditions and meanings that make a company unique.

a. Merit Shop
b. Graduate recruitment
c. Corporate culture
d. Cross-functional team

5. _____ is an idea in the field of Organizational studies and management which describes the psychology, attitudes, experiences, beliefs and Values (personal and cultural values) of an organization. It has been defined as 'the specific collection of values and norms that are shared by people and groups in an organization and that control the way they interact with each other and with stakeholders outside the organization.'

This definition continues to explain organizational values also known as 'beliefs and ideas about what kinds of goals members of an organization should pursue and ideas about the appropriate kinds or standards of behavior organizational members should use to achieve these goals. From organizational values develop organizational norms, guidelines or expectations that prescribe appropriate kinds of behavior by employees in particular situations and control the behavior of organizational members towards one another.'

_____ is not the same as corporate culture.

a. AAAI
b. Organizational culture
c. A Stake in the Outcome
d. A4e

Chapter 11. Characteristics of the Situation

6. _____ or industrialization in North America, is the process of social and economic change whereby a human group is transformed from a pre-industrial society into an industrial one. It is a part of a wider modernisation process, where social change and economic development are closely related with technological innovation, particularly with the development of large-scale energy and metallurgy production. It is the extensive organisation of an economy for the purpose of manufacturing.
   a. AAAI
   b. A4e
   c. A Stake in the Outcome
   d. Industrialistion

7. The _____, also commonly known as the Computer Age or Information Era, is an idea that the current age will be characterised by the ability of individuals to transfer information freely, and to have instant access to knowledge that would have been difficult or impossible to find previously. The idea is heavily linked to the concept of a Digital Age or Digital Revolution, and carries the ramifications of a shift from traditional industry that the Industrial Revolution brought through industrialisation, to an economy based around the manipulation of information. The period is generally said to have begun in the latter half of the 20th century, though the particular date varies.
   a. A Stake in the Outcome
   b. Information age
   c. AAAI
   d. A4e

8. A _____ is a list of the general tasks and responsibilities of a position. Typically, it also includes to whom the position reports, specifications such as the qualifications needed by the person in the job, salary range for the position, etc. A _____ is usually developed by conducting a job analysis, which includes examining the tasks and sequences of tasks necessary to perform the job.
   a. Job description
   b. Labour hire
   c. Recruitment
   d. Referral recruitment

9. _____ is, in very basic words, a position a firm occupies against its competitors.

According to Michael Porter, the three methods for creating a sustainable _____ are through:

1. Cost leadership - Cost advantage occurs when a firm delivers the same services as its competitors but at a lower cost;

2.

a. 28-hour day
b. 1990 Clean Air Act
c. 33 Strategies of War
d. Competitive advantage

10. In economics, the term _____ refers to situations where the advancement of a qualified person within the hierarchy of an organization is stopped at a lower level because of some form of discrimination, most commonly sexism or racism, but since the term was coined, '_____' has also come to describe the limited advancement of the deaf, blind, disabled, aged and sexual minorities.It is an unofficial, invisible barrier that prevents women and minorities from advancing in businesses.

This situation is referred to as a 'ceiling' as there is a limitation blocking upward advancement, and 'glass' (transparent) because the limitation is not immediately apparent and is normally an unwritten and unofficial policy. This invisible barrier continues to exist, even though there are no explicit obstacles keeping minorities from acquiring advanced job positions - there are no advertisements that specifically say 'no minorities hired at this establishment', nor are there any formal orders that say 'minorities are not qualified' - but they do lie beneath the surface.

a. 1990 Clean Air Act
b. 28-hour day
c. 33 Strategies of War
d. Glass ceiling

11. A _____ in today's workforce is an individual that is valued for their ability to interpret information within a specific subject area. They will often advance the overall understanding of that subject through focused analysis, design and/or development. They use research skills to define problems and to identify alternatives.
a. Sole proprietorship
b. Personal management interview
c. Knowledge worker
d. Cultural Intelligence

12. A 'supply chain is the system of organizations, people, technology, activities, information and resources involved in moving a product or service from _____ to customer. Supply chain activities transform natural resources, raw materials and components into a finished product that is delivered to the end customer. In sophisticated supply chain systems, used products may re-enter the supply chain at any point where residual value is recyclable.

a. National Examination Board in Occupational Safety and Health
b. Corrosive material
c. Supplier
d. Labor disputes

13. The sociologist Max Weber defined _____ as 'resting on devotion to the exceptional sanctity, heroism or exemplary character of an individual person, and of the normative patterns or order revealed or ordained by him.' _____ is one of three forms of authority laid out in Weber's tripartite classification of authority, the other two being traditional authority and rational-legal authority. The concept has acquired wide usage among sociologists.

In his writings about _____, Weber applies the term charisma to 'a certain quality of an individual personality, by virtue of which he is set apart from ordinary men and treated as endowed with supernatural, superhuman, or at least specifically exceptional powers or qualities.

a. 33 Strategies of War
b. Charismatic authority
c. 28-hour day
d. 1990 Clean Air Act

14. An _____ is a social arrangement which pursues collective goals, which controls its own performance, and which has a boundary separating it from its environment. The word itself is derived from the Greek word ά½„ργανον (organon [itself derived from the better-known word ά¼"ργον ergon - work; deed - > ergonomics, etc]) meaning tool. The term is used in both daily and scientific English in multiple ways.

a. Enron Corporation
b. Organization
c. American Psychological Society
d. Investment

15. A _____ is the learned capacity to carry out pre-determined results often with the minimum outlay of time, energy, or both. _____s can often be divided into domain-general and domain-specific _____s. For example, in the domain of work, some general _____s would include time management, teamwork and leadership, self motivation and others, whereas domain-specific _____s would be useful only for a certain job.

a. 28-hour day
b. 33 Strategies of War
c. 1990 Clean Air Act
d. Skill

16. _____ is a concept found in moral, political, and bioethical philosophy. Within these contexts, it refers to the capacity of a rational individual to make an informed, un-coerced decision. In moral and political philosophy, _____ is often used as the basis for determining moral responsibility for one's actions.

   a. A4e
   b. A Stake in the Outcome
   c. AAAI
   d. Autonomy

17. Hackman and Oldham proposed the _____, which is widely used as a framework to study how particular job characteristics impact on job outcomes, including job satisfaction. The model states that there are five core job characteristics (skill variety, task identity, task significance, autonomy, and feedback) which impact three critical psychological states (experienced meaningfulness, experienced responsibility for outcomes, and knowledge of the actual results), in turn influencing work outcomes (job satisfaction, absenteeism, work motivation, etc.).

   a. 33 Strategies of War
   b. 28-hour day
   c. Job Characteristics Model
   d. 1990 Clean Air Act

18. A _____ aims to describe aspects of a person's character that remain stable throughout that person's lifetime, the individual's character pattern of behavior, thoughts, and feelings. An early model of personality was posited by Greek philosopher/physician Hippocrates. The 20th century heralded a new interest in defining and identifying separate personality types, in close correlation with the emergence of the field of psychology.

   a. Picture Arrangement Test
   b. Morrisby Profile
   c. Taylor-Johnson Temperament Analysis
   d. Personality test

19. _____ is a dynamic of being mutually and physically responsible to and sharing a common set of principles with others. This concept differs distinctly from 'dependence' in that an interdependent relationship implies that all participants are emotionally, economically, ecologically and or morally 'interdependent.' Some people advocate freedom or independence as a sort of ultimate good; others do the same with devotion to one's family, community, or society. _____ recognizes the truth in each position and weaves them together.

   a. A Stake in the Outcome
   b. AAAI
   c. A4e
   d. Interdependence

20. _____ is a method of directing, instructing and training a person or group of people, with the aim to achieve some goal or develop specific skills. There are many ways to coach, types of _____ and methods to _____. Direction may include motivational speaking.

   a. 1990 Clean Air Act
   b. 28-hour day
   c. Coaching
   d. Co-coaching

21. The _____ captures an expanded spectrum of values and criteria for measuring organizational success: economic, ecological and social. With the ratification of the United Nations and ICLEI _____ standard for urban and community accounting in early 2007, this became the dominant approach to public sector full cost accounting. Similar UN standards apply to natural capital and human capital measurement to assist in measurements required by _____, e.g. the ecoBudget standard for reporting ecological footprint.

   a. 28-hour day
   b. 33 Strategies of War
   c. 1990 Clean Air Act
   d. Triple bottom line

22. _____ is a fixed set of rules of intra-organization procedures and structures. As such, it is usually set out in writing, with a language of rules that ostensibly leave little discretion for interpretation. In some societies and in some organization, such rules may be strictly followed; in others, they may be little more than an empty formalism.

   a. 33 Strategies of War
   b. 1990 Clean Air Act
   c. 28-hour day
   d. Formal organization

23. An _____ is a mostly hierarchical concept of subordination of entities that collaborate and contribute to serve one common aim.

Organizations are a variant of clustered entities. The structure of an organization is usually set up in many a styles, dependent on their objectives and ambience.

   a. AAAI
   b. A Stake in the Outcome
   c. A4e
   d. Organizational structure

Chapter 11. Characteristics of the Situation

24. _____ is the imitation of some real thing, state of affairs, or process. The act of simulating something generally entails representing certain key characteristics or behaviours of a selected physical or abstract system.

_____ is used in many contexts, including the modeling of natural systems or human systems in order to gain insight into their functioning.

 a. 33 Strategies of War
 b. Simulation
 c. 1990 Clean Air Act
 d. 28-hour day

25. _____ is the process by which the activities of an organization, particularly those regarding decision-making, become concentrated within a particular location and/or group.

In political science, this refers to the concentration of a government's power - both geographically and politically, into a centralized government.

 a. Task management
 b. Process Hazard Analysis
 c. Centralization
 d. Value-based

26. In formal logic, a _____ consists of a formal language together with a deductive system which consists of a set of inference rules and/or axioms. A _____ is used to derive one expression from one or more other expressions antecedently expressed in the system. These expressions are called axioms, in the case of those previously supposed to be true, or theorems, in the case of those derived.
 a. Retroduction
 b. Formal system
 c. Fallacy
 d. Testable

27. _____ is a paradigm used to simplify the design of hardware and software devices such as computer software and increasingly, 3D models. A _____ assures that each modular part of a device has only one responsibility and performs that responsibility with the minimum of side effects on other parts. Functionally-designed modules tend to have low coupling.

a. National War Labor Board
b. Zion National Park
c. National Institute for Occupational Safety and Health
d. Functional design

28. _____ can be defined as the idea generation, concept development, testing and manufacturing or implementation of a physical object or service. _____ers conceptualize and evaluate ideas, making them tangible through products in a more systematic approach. The role of a _____er encompasses many characteristics of the marketing manager, product manager, industrial designer and design engineer.
    a. Abraham Harold Maslow
    b. Adam Smith
    c. Affiliation
    d. Product design

29. The _____ is the interlocking social structure that governs how people work together in practice. It is the aggregate of behaviors, interactions, norms, personal and professional connections through which work gets done and relationships are built among people who share a common organizational affiliation or cluster of affiliations. It consists of a dynamic set of personal relationships, social networks, communities of common interest, and emotional sources of motivation.
    a. A4e
    b. AAAI
    c. A Stake in the Outcome
    d. Informal organization

30. _____ is a set of properties of the work environment, perceived directly or indirectly by employees, that is assumed to be a major force in influencing employee behavior. (Organizational Behavior ' Management, 8th Ed., Ivancevich, Konopaske, and Matteson)

A Queensland University of Technology view on _____...

The concept of _____ has been assessed by various authors, of which many of them published their own definition of organisational climate.

    a. Affiliation
    b. Organizational climate
    c. Abraham Harold Maslow
    d. Adam Smith

Chapter 11. Characteristics of the Situation

31. An _____ is a natural person, business, or corporation which provides goods or services to another entity under terms specified in a contract or within a verbal agreement. Unlike an employee, an _____ does not work regularly for an employer but works as and when required, during which time she or he may be subject to the Law of Agency. _____s are usually paid on a freelance basis.
    a. Occupational Safety and Health Act
    b. Offices, Shops and Railway Premises Act 1963
    c. Americans with Disabilities Act
    d. Independent contractor

32. More recently organizations have come to understand that leadership can also be developed by strengthening the connection between and alignment of the efforts of individual leaders and the systems through which they influence organizational operations. This has led to a differentiation between leader development and _____. Leader development focuses on the development of the leader, such as the personal attributes desired in a leader, desired ways of behaving, ways of thinking or feeling.
    a. Pseudoconsensus
    b. Leadership development
    c. Path-goal theory
    d. Group process consultation

33. _____ is a leadership style that defines as leadership that creates voluble and positive change in the followers. A transformational leader focuses on 'transforming' others to help each other, to look out for each other, be encouraging, harmonious, and look out for the organization as a whole. In this leadership, the leader enhances the motivation, moral and performance of his follower group.
    a. Milgram experiment
    b. Need for affiliation
    c. Transformational leadership
    d. Subpersonality

Chapter 12. Contingency Theories of Leadership

1. _____ is the state achieved by coming together, the state of agreement. The Latin congruere means to come together, agree. As an abstract term, _____ means similarity between objects.
   a. Turnover
   b. HMIS
   c. Congruence
   d. The Goodyear Tire ' Rubber Company

2. _____ is a class of behavioural theory that claims that there is no best way to organize a corporation, to lead a company, or to make decisions. Instead, the optimal course of action is contingent (dependant) upon the internal and external situation. Several contingency approaches were developed concurrently in the late 1960s.
   a. Resource-based view
   b. Contingency Theory
   c. Goal setting
   d. Senior management

3. _____ is a kind of action that occurs as two or more objects have an effect upon one another. The idea of a two-way effect is essential in the concept of _____, as opposed to a one-way causal effect. A closely related term is interconnectivity, which deals with the _____s of _____s within systems: combinations of many simple _____s can lead to surprising emergent phenomena.
   a. Interaction
   b. Interpersonal communication
   c. Organizational communication
   d. Organizational dissent

4. An _____ is a form of government in which the political power is held by a single, self-appointed ruler. The term autocrat is derived from the Greek word 'αυτοκρÎ¬τωρ . Compare with oligarchy ('rule by the few') and democracy ('rule by the people'.)
   a. AAAI
   b. A4e
   c. Autocracy
   d. A Stake in the Outcome

5. A _____ or chief executive is one of the highest-ranking corporate officer (executive) or administrator in charge of total management. An individual selected as President and _____ of a corporation, company, organization, or agency, reports to the board of directors. In internal communication and press releases, many companies capitalize the term and those of other high positions, even when they are not proper nouns.

Chapter 12. Contingency Theories of Leadership

a. Questionnaire
b. Bandwagon effect
c. Learning
d. Chief executive officer

6. A _____ is a decision support tool that uses a tree-like graph or model of decisions and their possible consequences, including chance event outcomes, resource costs, and utility. _____s are commonly used in operations research, specifically in decision analysis, to help identify a strategy most likely to reach a goal. Another use of _____s is as a descriptive means for calculating conditional probabilities.
   a. 33 Strategies of War
   b. 28-hour day
   c. 1990 Clean Air Act
   d. Decision tree

7. _____ is the set of reasons that determines one to engage in a particular behavior. The term is generally used for human _____ but, theoretically, it can be used to describe the causes for animal behavior as well
   a. Losada line
   b. Losada Zone
   c. Motivation
   d. Work behavior

8. _____ is a behavior which is characterized by deferment of actions or tasks to a later time. Psychologists often cite _____ as a mechanism for coping with the anxiety associated with starting or completing any task or decision. Psychology researchers also have three criteria they use to categorize _____.
   a. 33 Strategies of War
   b. Procrastination
   c. 1990 Clean Air Act
   d. 28-hour day

9. The _____ is a leadership theory in the field of organizational studies developed by Robert House in 1971 and revised in 1996. The theory that a leader's behavior is contingent to the satisfaction, motivation and performance of subordinates. The revised version also argues that the leader engage in behaviors that complement subordinate's abilities and compensate for deficiencies.

a. Path-goal theory
b. Job analysis
c. Work design
d. Leadership development

10. The sociologist Max Weber defined _____ as 'resting on devotion to the exceptional sanctity, heroism or exemplary character of an individual person, and of the normative patterns or order revealed or ordained by him.' _____ is one of three forms of authority laid out in Weber's tripartite classification of authority, the other two being traditional authority and rational-legal authority. The concept has acquired wide usage among sociologists.

In his writings about _____, Weber applies the term charisma to 'a certain quality of an individual personality, by virtue of which he is set apart from ordinary men and treated as endowed with supernatural, superhuman, or at least specifically exceptional powers or qualities.

a. 33 Strategies of War
b. 28-hour day
c. 1990 Clean Air Act
d. Charismatic authority

11. _____ is a term used to classify a group leadership theories that inquire the interactions between leaders and followers. A transactional leader focuses more on a series of 'transactions'. This person is interested in looking out for oneself, having exchange benefits with their subordinates and clarify a sense of duty with rewards and punishments to reach goals.
a. Reflective listening
b. Negative affectivity
c. Care perspective
d. Transactional leadership

12. _____ is a leadership style that defines as leadership that creates voluble and positive change in the followers. A transformational leader focuses on 'transforming' others to help each other, to look out for each other, be encouraging, harmonious, and look out for the organization as a whole. In this leadership, the leader enhances the motivation, moral and performance of his follower group.
a. Need for affiliation
b. Transformational leadership
c. Milgram experiment
d. Subpersonality

13. Social _____ is a social psychological and sociological perspective that explains social change and stability as a process of negotiated exchanges between parties. Social _____ posits that all human relationships are formed by the use of a subjective cost-benefit analysis and the comparison of alternatives. For example, when a person perceives the costs of a relationship as outweighing the perceived benefits, then the theory predicts that the person will choose to leave the relationship.

   a. AAAI
   b. A Stake in the Outcome
   c. A4e
   d. Exchange theory

14. Leadership is one of the primary areas of study, research, and practice in organizational behavior. Leaders often develop relationships with each member of the group that they lead, and _____ explains how those relationships with various members can develop in unique ways.

The _____ of leadership focuses on the two-way relationship between supervisors and subordinates.

   a. Light curtains
   b. Groups decision making
   c. Human Centered Systems
   d. Leader-Member Exchange theory

15. _____ is a term in psychology which refers to a person's belief about what causes the good or bad results in his or her life, either in general or in a specific area such as health or academics. Understanding of the concept was developed by Julian B. Rotter in 1954, and has since become an important aspect of personality studies.

_____ refers to the extent to which individuals believe that they can control events that affect them.

   a. Dump job
   b. Locus of control
   c. Social identity theory
   d. Developmental profile

Chapter 13. Leadership and Change

1. The sociologist Max Weber defined _____ as 'resting on devotion to the exceptional sanctity, heroism or exemplary character of an individual person, and of the normative patterns or order revealed or ordained by him.' _____ is one of three forms of authority laid out in Weber's tripartite classification of authority, the other two being traditional authority and rational-legal authority. The concept has acquired wide usage among sociologists.

   In his writings about _____, Weber applies the term charisma to 'a certain quality of an individual personality, by virtue of which he is set apart from ordinary men and treated as endowed with supernatural, superhuman, or at least specifically exceptional powers or qualities.

   a. 33 Strategies of War
   b. 1990 Clean Air Act
   c. 28-hour day
   d. Charismatic authority

2. _____ is a term used to classify a group leadership theories that inquire the interactions between leaders and followers. A transactional leader focuses more on a series of 'transactions'. This person is interested in looking out for oneself, having exchange benefits with their subordinates and clarify a sense of duty with rewards and punishments to reach goals.
   a. Care perspective
   b. Transactional leadership
   c. Reflective listening
   d. Negative affectivity

3. _____ is a leadership style that defines as leadership that creates voluble and positive change in the followers. A transformational leader focuses on 'transforming' others to help each other, to look out for each other, be encouraging, harmonious, and look out for the organization as a whole. In this leadership, the leader enhances the motivation, moral and performance of his follower group.
   a. Milgram experiment
   b. Transformational leadership
   c. Subpersonality
   d. Need for affiliation

4. _____ Stores, Inc. is an American public corporation that runs a chain of large, discount department stores. It is the world's largest public corporation by revenue, according to the 2008 Fortune Global 500.
   a. Abraham Harold Maslow
   b. Adam Smith
   c. Wal-Mart
   d. William Edwards Deming

Chapter 13. Leadership and Change

5. _____ is any process of estimating or inferring how local policies, actions, or changes influences the state of the neighboring universe. It is an approach to problem solving that views 'problems' as parts of an overall system, rather than reacting to present outcomes or events and potentially contributing to further development of the undesired issue or problem. _____ is a framework that is based on the belief that the component parts of a system can best be understood in the context of relationships with each other and with other systems, rather than in isolation.

   a. Sociotechnical systems theory
   b. Systems thinking
   c. Subsystems
   d. Systems theory

6. A _____ or objective is a projected state of affairs that a person or a system plans or intends to achieve--a personal or organizational desired end-point in some sort of assumed development. Many people endeavor to reach _____s within a finite time by setting deadlines.

   A desire or an intention becomes a _____ if and only if one activates an action for achieving it

   a. Goal
   b. Span of control
   c. Management by exception
   d. Task list

7. Organizations sometimes summarize goals and objectives into a mission statement and/or a _____:

   While the existence of a shared mission is extremely useful, many strategy specialists question the requirement for a written mission statement. However, there are many models of strategic planning that start with mission statements, so it is useful to examine them here.

   - A Mission statement tells you the fundamental purpose of the organization. It concentrates on the present. It defines the customer and the critical processes. It informs you of the desired level of performance.

   - A _____ outlines what the organization wants to be. It concentrates on the future.

   a. 33 Strategies of War
   b. 28-hour day
   c. 1990 Clean Air Act
   d. Vision statement

Chapter 13. Leadership and Change

8. _____ is the practice of imposing something unpleasant or aversive on a person or animal, usually in response to disobedience, defiance governmental which is recorded in English since 1340, deriving from Old French puniss-, an extended form of the stem of punir 'to punish,' from Latin punire 'inflict a penalty on, cause pain for some offense,' earlier poenire, from poena 'penalty, _____ of great loss'.

Colloquial use of to punish for 'to inflict heavy damage or loss' is first recorded in 1801, originally in boxing; for punishing as 'hard-hitting' is from 1811.

   a. 28-hour day
   b. 33 Strategies of War
   c. 1990 Clean Air Act
   d. Punishment

9. _____ is the state achieved by coming together, the state of agreement. The Latin congruere means to come together, agree. As an abstract term, _____ means similarity between objects.
   a. HMIS
   b. The Goodyear Tire ' Rubber Company
   c. Turnover
   d. Congruence

10. Social _____ is a social psychological and sociological perspective that explains social change and stability as a process of negotiated exchanges between parties. Social _____ posits that all human relationships are formed by the use of a subjective cost-benefit analysis and the comparison of alternatives. For example, when a person perceives the costs of a relationship as outweighing the perceived benefits, then the theory predicts that the person will choose to leave the relationship.
   a. A Stake in the Outcome
   b. A4e
   c. AAAI
   d. Exchange theory

11. Leadership is one of the primary areas of study, research, and practice in organizational behavior. Leaders often develop relationships with each member of the group that they lead, and _____ explains how those relationships with various members can develop in unique ways.

The _____ of leadership focuses on the two-way relationship between supervisors and subordinates.

a. Human Centered Systems
b. Groups decision making
c. Leader-Member Exchange theory
d. Light curtains

12. _____ is an influential development in the field of social science. It provides a framework for looking at the factors (forces) that influence a situation, originally social situations. It looks at forces that are either driving movement toward a goal (helping forces) or blocking movement toward a goal (hindering forces.)
    a. Performance improvement
    b. Force field analysis
    c. Resource-based view
    d. Goal setting

13. In psychology, the 'Big Five' personality traits are five broad factors or dimensions of personality developed through lexical analysis. This is the rational and statistical analysis of words related to personality as found in natural-language dictionaries. The traits are also referred to as the '_____'.
    a. Behaviorism
    b. Groupthink
    c. Conformity
    d. Five Factor Model

14. A _____ is a research instrument consisting of a series of questions and other prompts for the purpose of gathering information from respondents. Although they are often designed for statistical analysis of the responses, this is not always the case. The _____ was invented by Sir Francis Galton.
    a. 28-hour day
    b. 1990 Clean Air Act
    c. Structured interview
    d. Questionnaire

15. _____ is the art of using language as a means to persuade. Along with grammar and logic or dialectic, _____ is one of the three ancient arts of discourse. From ancient Greece to the late 19th Century, it was a central part of Western education, filling the need to train public speakers and writers to move audiences to action with arguments.
    a. 28-hour day
    b. 1990 Clean Air Act
    c. 33 Strategies of War
    d. Rhetoric

Chapter 13. Leadership and Change

16. A _____ is the learned capacity to carry out pre-determined results often with the minimum outlay of time, energy, or both. _____s can often be divided into domain-general and domain-specific _____s. For example, in the domain of work, some general _____s would include time management, teamwork and leadership, self motivation and others, whereas domain-specific _____s would be useful only for a certain job.
   a. 28-hour day
   b. 33 Strategies of War
   c. 1990 Clean Air Act
   d. Skill

17. In the arts and antiques, _____ is the judgment by experts as to the authorship, date, or other aspect of the origin of a work of art or cultural artifact. Works 'attributed' to an artist are more firmly believed to be theirs than those 'ascribed'.

   _____ can also mean:

   - _____, a concept in copyright law requiring an author to be credited
   - Journalism sourcing (or _____), a journalistic practice of attributing information to its source
   - _____ (psychology), a concept in psychology whereby people attribute traits and causes to things they observe
   - Performance _____, a technique in quantitative finance for explaining the active performance of a portfolio

   a. A Stake in the Outcome
   b. Ambition
   c. A4e
   d. Attribution

18. _____ is the set of reasons that determines one to engage in a particular behavior. The term is generally used for human _____ but, theoretically, it can be used to describe the causes for animal behavior as well
   a. Work behavior
   b. Losada line
   c. Losada Zone
   d. Motivation

19. _____ refers to increasing the spiritual, political, social or economic strength of individuals and communities. It often involves the empowered developing confidence in their own capacities.

Chapter 13. Leadership and Change

The term Human _____ covers a vast landscape of meanings, interpretations, definitions and disciplines ranging from psychology and philosophy to the highly commercialized Self-Help industry and Motivational sciences.

a. Emotional labor
b. Institutionalisation
c. Institutionalization
d. Empowerment

20. _____ is a dynamic of being mutually and physically responsible to and sharing a common set of principles with others. This concept differs distinctly from 'dependence' in that an interdependent relationship implies that all participants are emotionally, economically, ecologically and or morally 'interdependent.' Some people advocate freedom or independence as a sort of ultimate good; others do the same with devotion to one's family, community, or society. _____ recognizes the truth in each position and weaves them together.

a. A4e
b. AAAI
c. Interdependence
d. A Stake in the Outcome

21. A _____ is a social structure made of nodes (which are generally individuals or organizations) that are tied by one or more specific types of interdependency, such as values, visions, ideas, financial exchange, friendship, sexual relationships, kinship, dislike, conflict or trade.

_____ analysis views social relationships in terms of nodes and ties. Nodes are the individual actors within the networks, and ties are the relationships between the actors.

a. Diversity training
b. Reference group
c. Social influence
d. Social network

22. _____ involves establishing specific, measurable and time-targeted objectives. Work on the theory of goal-setting suggests that it's an effective tool for making progress by ensuring that participants in a group with a common goal are clearly aware of what is expected from them if an objective is to be achieved. On a personal level, setting goals is a process that allows people to specify then work towards their own objectives - most commonly with financial or career-based goals.

a. Management Development
b. Theory X and theory Y
c. Best practice
d. Goal setting

23. _____ describes the situation when output from (or information about the result of) an event or phenomenon in the past will influence the same event/phenomenon in the present or future. When an event is part of a chain of cause-and-effect that forms a circuit or loop, then the event is said to 'feed back' into itself.

_____ is also a synonym for:

- _____ Signal; the information about the initial event that is the basis for subsequent modification of the event.
- _____ Loop; the causal path that leads from the initial generation of the _____ signal to the subsequent modification of the event.

_____ is a mechanism, process or signal that is looped back to control a system within itself. Such a loop is called a _____ loop.

a. Feedback
b. 28-hour day
c. 1990 Clean Air Act
d. Positive feedback

24. _____ also known as protocols, are the instant written record of a meeting or hearing. They often give an overview of the structure of the meeting, starting with a list of those present, a statement of the various issues before the participants, and each of their responses thereto. They are often created at the moment of the hearing by a typist or court recorder at the meeting, who may record the meeting in shorthand, and then prepare the _____ and issue them to the participants afterwards.

a. Keiretsu
b. Minutes
c. Trade union
d. Contingent work

25. _____ refers to the long-term management of intractable conflicts. It is the label for the variety of ways by which people handle grievances--standing up for what they consider to be right and against what they consider to be wrong. Those ways include such diverse phenomena as gossip, ridicule, lynching, terrorism, warfare, feuding, genocide, law, mediation, and avoidance.

a. 1990 Clean Air Act
b. 33 Strategies of War
c. Conflict management
d. 28-hour day

26. _____ is a recursive process where two or more people or organizations work together intersection of common goals -- for example, an intellectual endeavor that is creative in nature--by sharing knowledge, learning and building consensus. _____ does not require leadership and can sometimes bring better results through decentralization and egalitarianism. In particular, teams that work collaboratively can obtain greater resources, recognition and reward when facing competition for finite resources. _____ is also present in opposing goals exhibiting the notion of adversarial _____, though this notion is atypical of the annotation that people have given towards their understanding of _____.
   a. Collaboration
   b. Collectivism
   c. Mass collaboration
   d. Collaborative learning

27. _____ is a range of processes aimed at alleviating or eliminating sources of conflict. The term '_____' is sometimes used interchangeably with the term dispute resolution or alternative dispute resolution. Processes of _____ generally include negotiation, mediation and diplomacy.
   a. 28-hour day
   b. Conflict resolution
   c. 1990 Clean Air Act
   d. 33 Strategies of War

28. The _____ captures an expanded spectrum of values and criteria for measuring organizational success: economic, ecological and social. With the ratification of the United Nations and ICLEI _____ standard for urban and community accounting in early 2007, this became the dominant approach to public sector full cost accounting. Similar UN standards apply to natural capital and human capital measurement to assist in measurements required by _____, e.g. the ecoBudget standard for reporting ecological footprint.
   a. 28-hour day
   b. 33 Strategies of War
   c. 1990 Clean Air Act
   d. Triple bottom line

Chapter 13. Leadership and Change

29. In arguments, _____ is a concept of finding agreement through communication, through a mutual acceptance of terms--often involving variations from an original goal or desire. Extremism is often considered as antonym to _____, which, depending on context, may be associated with concepts of balance, tolerance. In the negative connotation, _____ may be referred to as capitulation, referring to a 'surrender' of objectives, principles, or materiale, in the process of negotiating an agreement.
    a. 28-hour day
    b. 1990 Clean Air Act
    c. 33 Strategies of War
    d. Compromise

30. _____ forms part of thinking. Considered the most complex of all intellectual functions, _____ has been defined as higher-order cognitive process that requires the modulation and control of more routine or fundamental skills. It occurs if an organism or an artificial intelligence system does not know how to proceed from a given state to a desired goal state.
    a. Thinking outside the box
    b. 1990 Clean Air Act
    c. Functional fixedness
    d. Problem solving

31. The _____ is a decision making method for use among groups of many sizes, who want to make their decision quickly, as by a vote, but want everyone's opinions taken into account (as opposed to traditional voting, where only the largest group is considered) . The method of tallying is the difference. First, every member of the group gives their view of the solution, with a short explanation.
    a. Stepladder technique
    b. Cost-benefit analysis
    c. 1990 Clean Air Act
    d. Nominal Group Technique

32. _____ is a group creativity technique designed to generate a large number of ideas for the solution of a problem. The method was first popularized in the late 1930s by Alex Faickney Osborn in a book called Applied Imagination. Osborn proposed that groups could double their creative output with _____.
    a. Abraham Harold Maslow
    b. Brainstorming
    c. Affiliation
    d. Adam Smith

33. _____ is a cognitive bias that limits a person to using an object only in the way it is traditionally used.

Chapter 13. Leadership and Change

The concept of _____ originated in Gestalt Psychology, which is a movement in psychology that emphasizes holistic processing where the whole is seen as being separate from the sum of its parts. Karl Duncker defined _____ as being a 'mental block against using an object in a new way that is required to solve a problem.' This 'block' then limits that ability of an individual to use the components given to them to make a specific item, as they can not move past the original intention of the object.

   a. Thinking outside the box
   b. Problem solving
   c. 1990 Clean Air Act
   d. Functional fixedness

34. A _____ aims to describe aspects of a person's character that remain stable throughout that person's lifetime, the individual's character pattern of behavior, thoughts, and feelings. An early model of personality was posited by Greek philosopher/physician Hippocrates. The 20th century heralded a new interest in defining and identifying separate personality types, in close correlation with the emergence of the field of psychology.
   a. Personality test
   b. Morrisby Profile
   c. Taylor-Johnson Temperament Analysis
   d. Picture Arrangement Test

35. A _____ or chief executive is one of the highest-ranking corporate officer (executive) or administrator in charge of total management. An individual selected as President and _____ of a corporation, company, organization, or agency, reports to the board of directors. In internal communication and press releases, many companies capitalize the term and those of other high positions, even when they are not proper nouns.
   a. Chief executive officer
   b. Bandwagon effect
   c. Learning
   d. Questionnaire

36. A _____ is directly responsible for managing the day-to-day operations (and profitability) of a company.

Chief Executive Officer (CEO)
   - As the top manager, the CEO is typically responsible for the entire operations of the corporation and reports directly to the chairman and board of directors. It is the CEO's responsibility to implement board decisions and initiatives and to maintain the smooth operation of the firm, with the assistance of senior management.

a. Force field analysis
b. Management by objectives
c. Senior management
d. Management team

37. An _____ is a mostly hierarchical concept of subordination of entities that collaborate and contribute to serve one common aim.

Organizations are a variant of clustered entities. The structure of an organization is usually set up in many a styles, dependent on their objectives and ambience.

a. Organizational structure
b. A4e
c. A Stake in the Outcome
d. AAAI

ANSWER KEY

Chapter 1
1. d 2. a 3. b 4. d

Chapter 2
1. d 2. c 3. d 4. d 5. c 6. a 7. b 8. d 9. d 10. d
11. c 12. b 13. a 14. b 15. d 16. d 17. d 18. d 19. c

Chapter 3
1. a 2. d 3. b 4. b 5. b 6. b 7. c 8. b 9. d 10. c
11. a 12. b 13. a 14. a 15. d 16. a 17. b 18. c 19. c 20. a
21. b 22. d

Chapter 4
1. b 2. d 3. a 4. c 5. c 6. d 7. a 8. d 9. b 10. d
11. c 12. d 13. b 14. c 15. d 16. b 17. b 18. d 19. d 20. d
21. d 22. a 23. b 24. a 25. a 26. d 27. d 28. a 29. d 30. d
31. b

Chapter 5
1. d 2. d 3. d 4. d 5. d 6. a 7. d 8. a 9. a 10. b
11. c 12. d 13. c 14. a 15. a 16. d

Chapter 6
1. a 2. c 3. b 4. d 5. c 6. b 7. a 8. a 9. c 10. d
11. a 12. d 13. d 14. b 15. d 16. d 17. a 18. d 19. d 20. d
21. b 22. d

Chapter 7
1. b 2. d 3. d 4. b 5. d 6. c 7. d 8. b 9. b 10. d
11. d 12. b 13. d 14. b 15. d 16. a 17. b 18. c 19. d 20. d
21. d 22. d 23. d 24. d 25. c

Chapter 8
1. d 2. d 3. d 4. d 5. c 6. a 7. d 8. b 9. d 10. d
11. b 12. c 13. d 14. c 15. d 16. b 17. d 18. b 19. d 20. a
21. b 22. d 23. d 24. d 25. a 26. c 27. d 28. d 29. b 30. c
31. a 32. c 33. d 34. b 35. d 36. d 37. d 38. a 39. d 40. d
41. c 42. c 43. b 44. d 45. d 46. d

Chapter 9
1. c 2. b 3. d 4. d 5. a 6. d 7. d 8. b 9. b 10. a
11. c 12. d 13. a 14. d 15. d 16. d 17. d 18. b 19. b 20. d
21. d 22. d 23. d 24. c 25. a 26. c 27. d 28. a 29. c 30. a
31. a 32. c 33. d 34. b 35. d 36. d 37. c 38. c 39. d 40. d
41. b 42. b 43. d 44. b 45. d

Chapter 10

1. b	2. d	3. d	4. d	5. c	6. d	7. d	8. d	9. c	10. c
11. d	12. c	13. d	14. a	15. d	16. d	17. d	18. c	19. d	20. d
21. d	22. a	23. d	24. b	25. c	26. d	27. c	28. d	29. d	30. d
31. a	32. b	33. d	34. d	35. b	36. d	37. c	38. c	39. c	40. d
41. a	42. c	43. d	44. a	45. d	46. d	47. a	48. c	49. b	50. a
51. d	52. c	53. a							

Chapter 11

1. a	2. d	3. a	4. c	5. b	6. d	7. b	8. a	9. d	10. d
11. c	12. c	13. b	14. b	15. d	16. d	17. c	18. d	19. d	20. c
21. d	22. d	23. d	24. b	25. c	26. b	27. d	28. d	29. d	30. b
31. d	32. b	33. c							

Chapter 12

1. c	2. b	3. a	4. c	5. d	6. d	7. c	8. b	9. a	10. d
11. d	12. b	13. d	14. d	15. b					

Chapter 13

1. d	2. b	3. b	4. c	5. b	6. a	7. d	8. d	9. d	10. d
11. c	12. b	13. d	14. d	15. d	16. d	17. d	18. d	19. d	20. c
21. d	22. d	23. a	24. b	25. c	26. a	27. b	28. d	29. d	30. d
31. d	32. b	33. d	34. a	35. a	36. d	37. a			

www.ingramcontent.com/pod-product-compliance
Lightning Source LLC
Chambersburg PA
CBHW081707140225
21980CB00012B/698